Jim Burke is among the finest writing educators we have ... search, instruction, students, and society and mines them f... formulate as instructional principles and activities that support students' writing, thinking, and learning. *The Six Academic Writing Assignments* is a groundbreaking amalgam of his work with his own students and the efforts of so many teachers with whom he has worked. It is phenomenal. Read it!

—JUDITH A. LANGER, Vincent O'Leary Distinguished
Research Professor, University at Albany

A new generation of high school teachers now write books as once only college professors did, and they write better ones—and with greater relevance to teaching—than most of those professors. To me Jim Burke is the leading figure in this emerging trend, and in this valuable new book he applies "the principles of design thinking" to writing assignments, "the secret operating systems of our classes," as he calls them, that, for better or worse, affect whether students "learn to write well for academic purposes."

—GERALD GRAFF, Professor of English and Education, University
of Illinois at Chicago, and author of *They Say, I Say*

In this impressive book, Jim Burke offers a deep and thoughtful look at why we do what we do in designing academic writing assignments, inspiring us to be mindful of the mental moves we want our students to engage in and intentional in creating intellectual experiences to teach and transform them. At once theoretical and practical, this book is filled with a rich array of user-friendly, classroom-tested practices teachers can use to map out a yearlong writing journey for their students.

—CAROL BOOTH OLSON, Professor of Education, University of California,
Irvine, and author of *The Reading-Writing Connection*

Using innovative tenets of design thinking, Burke deeply empathizes with students as they try to use the course material teachers design for them. This level of empathy allows him (and us) to focus more effectively on the actual learning *experiences* of students as they confront assignments. Rich with online resources, examples of real student work, and pages upon pages of ideas and problem-solving advice, *The Six Academic Writing Assignments* provides expert and sage guidance. In his friendly, wise, and inimitably readable voice, Burke encourages teachers of all subjects to better reflect on and improve the ways they direct and guide their own students as writers.

—KEN LINDBLOM, coauthor of *Making the Journey*, Fourth Edition,
and former editor of NCTE's *English Journal*

This book demystifies the complexities of what we ask students to write. Creating assignments for our students is one of the most important moves in our teaching repertoires, and Jim Burke shines a light on what to consider—more than most students would probably ever imagine. Leave it to Burke to help us all improve our teaching craft through sharing concrete ways to gauge abstract processes.

—GRETCHEN BERNABEI, author of *The Story of My Thinking*

The 6 Academic Writing Assignments

JIM BURKE

The **6** **Academic Writing** Assignments

Designing the User's Journey

HEINEMANN
Portsmouth, NH

Heinemann
361 Hanover Street
Portsmouth, NH 03801–3912
www.heinemann.com

Offices and agents throughout the world

> *The author has dedicated a great deal of time and effort to writing the content of this book, and his written expression is protected by copyright law. We respectfully ask that you do not adapt, reuse, or copy anything on third-party (whether for-profit or not-for-profit) lesson-sharing websites. As always, we're happy to answer any questions you may have.*
>
> **—Heinemann Publishers**

"Dedicated to Teachers" is a trademark of Greenwood Publishing Group, Inc.

The author and publisher wish to thank those who have generously given permission to reprint borrowed material:

Excerpts from "Reversing Readicide" by Kelly Gallagher from *Educational Leadership*, Volume 67, Number 6, March 2010. Copyright © 2010 by the Association for Supervision and Curriculum Development. Reprinted by permission of the Copyright Clearance Center.

Credits for borrowed material continue on p. xiii.

Library of Congress Cataloging-in-Publication Data
Name: Burke, Jim, author.
Title: The six academic writing assignments : designing the user's journey / Jim Burke.
Description: Portsmouth, NH : Heinemann, 2019. | Includes bibliographical references.
Identifiers: LCCN 2018020078 | ISBN 9780325050942
Subjects: LCSH: English language—Composition and exercises—Study and teaching (Secondary) | English language—Composition and exercises—Study and teaching (Higher) | Report writing—Study and teaching (Secondary) | Report writing—Study and teaching (Higher)
Classification: LCC LB1631 .B77385 2019 | DDC 428.0071/2—dc23

LC record available at https://lccn.loc.gov/2018020078

Acquisitions Editors: Tom Newkirk and Sue Paro
Production Editor: Sean Moreau
Cover Designer: Monica Crigler
Interior Designer: Kim Arney
Typesetter: Kim Arney
Manufacturing: Steve Bernier

Printed in the United States of America on acid-free paper
22 21 20 19 18   CGB   1 2 3 4 5

Ever grateful for my students and colleagues at Burlingame High School, and for all that they have taught me these many years.

Contents

The Six Academic Writing Assignments Online Resources

To access the online resources for *The Six Academic Writing Assignments*, either scan this QR code or visit hein.pub/6AcademicAssignments-login. Enter your email address and password (or click "Create New Account" to set up an account). Once you have logged in, enter keycode **SIXDESIGN** and click "Register."

Online Resource Contents

Chapter Four

Chapter Five

Chapter Six

Conclusion

Acknowledgments

This book about writing taught me more about writing, especially writing as a process, than any other book I have ever written. Over the course of five years, I wrote at least three different versions of this book, each time realizing what I had learned along the way and why that latest version was not the book I was trying to write. Fortunately, I had editors and others at Heinemann who demonstrated their faith in me, the book, and the writing process at every step. Specifically, Tobey Antao helped me get started and guided me through the early stages of my thinking. Eventually, Tom Newkirk joined the conversation and, along with Sue Paro, accompanied me through the remaining drafts, listening, recommending, and always helping me to hear the recurring ideas that I was often slow to notice.

When I began to wonder if I had forgotten how to write books or if I would ever finish this one, the generous leaders and cooler heads at Heinemann prevailed. Thus, deepest thanks to Patty Adams, Kim Arney, Cindy Black, Vicki Boyd, Kim Cahill, Eric Chalek, Monica Crigler, Michelle Flynn, Sarah Fournier, Lisa Fowler, Sean Moreau, Edie Davis Quinn, and Elizabeth Tripp. Though Heinemann's credo is "Dedicated to Teachers," the truth is that the company is just as dedicated to its writers, something I have come to understand and appreciate more and more over the twenty years I have worked with all the wonderful people there.

When I had ideas I needed to try out or early versions of the book I wanted to get a response to, the colleagues I have come to trust and value so much over the years when it comes to academic writing were always generous with their time and responses: Gretchen Barnebei, Kelly Gallagher, Carol Jago, Penny Kittle, Carol Booth Olson, Laura Robb, Michael Smith, and Jeff Wilhelm. Two people merit special mention, for reasons we should all understand: Arthur Applebee and Judith Langer. Over the five years during which I wrote this book, I returned constantly to their work, especially their last book together, *Writing Instruction That Works: Proven Methods for Middle and High School Classrooms* (2013). However, I have always been grateful for the friendship and mentorship both Judith and Arthur provided me from my earliest days as a writer. In one way or another, this book stands as a testimony to all that I have learned from their writings, our conversations, and their example over the years. When I learned of Arthur's death in 2015, I could only think of his exemplary career as a scholar who had, from the moment I began to write, been willing to take me seriously and respond to my queries so thoughtfully in the mad scrum following their sessions at the National Council of Teachers of English (NCTE) annual conference or over a nice dinner with him and Judith while visiting them in Albany.

During the five years I spent grappling with this book, my wife, Susan, was never anything but what she has been since the earliest days of my writing: supportive, helpful, and patient. Three summers in a row, each of which I devoted almost entirely to writing this book, culminated in me declaring, with great confidence each time, that I had finally finished the book—only to realize by the time I had sent it off to my editors that I had still not found the core of the ideas. During those same years, I taught at Burlingame High School, where I have worked now for over twenty-five years. There, teaching seniors year in and year out, trying to cope with the changes and challenges that greet us every new year, I have learned more than any one book can possibly hold; my students remain, as the dedication shows, my most important teachers, though the lessons I learn from them are perhaps more by accident than by design.

Finally, this book more than any other reflects all that I have learned from teachers such as yourself, for over the last five years I have gathered, studied, thought about, and gained invaluable lessons from the hundreds and hundreds of writing assignments I have collected from teachers around the country and used to identify the lessons I am excited to share with you in the book that follows.

Introduction
Designing the User's Journey

Friction refers to anything that prevents a user from accomplishing a goal. Friction weighs down interactions, making even the most well-designed interfaces a nightmare to use. . . . [So] your goal is to create interactions which unravel with a natural sense of order and logic.

—JERRY CAO, "How to Reduce Friction with Good Design"

Epiphanies in the Copy Room

One morning, while standing amid the gaggle of my restless colleagues in the copy room, waiting my turn and hoping the copy machine would not break down before I got my handouts copied, I began looking at the different handouts stacked on the counter. Ranging from an inch high to over a foot tall, the towers of handouts represented the best efforts of teachers to prepare students for the exams, careers, colleges, and demands that awaited them as future citizens and consumers. As colleagues engaged in the usual pregame chatter, students shuffled past the copy room on their way to the classes where they would work with these same teachers, some of them new, others with years of experience—and all of us struggling to meet the many different expectations and challenges that came from all sides in familiar and ever-changing forms.

While casually looking over one handout, I had the rather obvious epiphany that these documents, whether we display them on screens or distribute them on paper, are the secret operating systems of our classes, for these are the instruments we put into students' hands. One handout I studied raised complicated questions for me that had serious implications. What assumptions do we make about our students—about their needs, interests, abilities, and knowledge? I started looking at the handouts around me more closely—the writing itself, the readability and usability of the documents, the appearance, conventions, and condition of them. I wondered if some of these features had different effects on students who struggled with learning difficulties or were still learning English. I began to wonder how the disinterested, failing student I was in high school (I graduated near the bottom of my class) would respond to some of the assignments I saw, as I looked at still other handouts while waiting to copy my own, which I had worked late the previous night to finish for class that day. I thought about similar assignments my own three children, having recently completed high school, had received. Some we had worked on for hours together to finish (Chaucer in a public school seventh-grade class where most parents spoke Chinese and Russian—seriously?). Others I had offered to help with, only to cause distress I could not have foreseen. ("But if you do that, it will be a *nine-sentence* paragraph and it has to be an *eight-sentence* paragraph!" my son lamented the one time when he let me help him with an English paper in middle school.) Other assignments I simply did not understand and could offer no help with, while many were, of course, perfectly reasonable and sound assignments.

Yet I also realize that we teach in a new and very different era from the one I encountered when I first entered the classroom. State standards. The rapid growth of Advanced Placement (AP) courses. The pressure to use and create more assignments for students to complete on the computers that now reside in so many (but not all) classrooms. Thus, many of the assignments I saw in the copy room will be, with increasing frequency, redesigned to be displayed and done on computer screens. They will not, of course, be better or more effective merely because they have been transformed into Google Docs or distributed through Google Classroom or a learning management system like Canvas, the latest solution to all problems that my district is requiring us to learn and use.

I was, without initially realizing it that day in the copy room, embarking on what Tom Newkirk describes as a "cycle of true research [in which we] take something [we] think we 'know'—and through sustained attention, begin to see it anew . . . to make the familiar strange" (2016, 8). What was made strange on that day was not only my own role as a teacher but also students themselves and the materials I designed for them to use. Over the next three years, I gathered hundreds of assignments from teachers and schools around the country, examining the various forms, features, and functions of these assignments. As a result, I came to understand that (1) our students are *users*—of our courses, materials, texts, and tools—whom we must understand and (2) we are *designers* who are charged with the task of removing from their journey through our curriculum what designers call "friction points" that can undermine students' learning and performance.

After that morning in the copy room, I began to see our work as designing not units and handouts, but experiences that, through the principles of design thinking, could be made more effective, more engaging, more instructive.

The designer Henry Dreyfuss captures this notion of the teacher as designer when he says that, whenever we design something, we must

> bear in mind that the object being worked on is going to be ridden in, sat upon, looked at, talked into, activated, operated or in some other way used by people. When the point of contact between the product and the people becomes a point of friction, then the [designer] has failed. On the other hand, if people are made safer, more efficient, more comfortable—or just plain happier—by contact with the product, then the designer has succeeded. (Adhikary 2009)

While Dreyfuss might be thinking about designing phones or chairs, books or bookcases, his point applies no less to the assignments and assessments, the handouts and digital documents we create for our students. The poorly designed handout, the incomprehensible directions, the overwhelmingly complex online app we thought we would use to make a simple task more interesting—these all come with their own friction points that affect students' ability to use the documents for their intended purpose: to help students learn in general and, in the context of this book, to learn to write well for academic purposes.

The Six Academic Writing Assignments We All Use

It was with all these thoughts in mind about design thinking that I began to focus on the writing assignments we create for our students. Not just the prompts. Not just the questions. Not the genres as we routinely think of them, but the actual types of writing themselves and the design of those assignments, whether on paper or a screen. When I finished my journey through the eighteen-inch pile of academic writing assignments I had amassed along the way, I discovered that our writing assignments, whether in English classes, social studies, science, or any other class, fall into six categories.

See Gordon Harvey's "A Brief Guide to the Elements of the Academic Essay" for an excellent, concise overview of academic writing.

Overview of the Six Major Academic Writing Assignments

1. *Writing to Learn:* Writing to learn (WTL) can be part of one's writing process (e.g., writing to generate ideas or discover connections); however, it can also be used to make sense of what students read, view, or listen to. WTL is an informal type of writing often done in a notebook, while taking notes, or following the

conventions of a specific discipline (e.g., scientific lab notes). WTL assignments tend to emphasize the thinking and content more than the style or quality of the writing.

2. *Short-Answer Writing:* Short-answer (SA) assignments range from one sentence to a paragraph. Though they appear on exams, they are also a constant on most homework and in-class assignments. They tend to ask students to explain or identify; some SA writing assignments follow the says–means–matters (SMM) format or an abbreviated version of the claim–reasoning–evidence (CRE) format. Such assignments emphasize content over style or quality of the writing, though there are inevitable exceptions, especially in English classes.

3. *Writing on Demand:* Writing-on-demand (WOD) assignments (a.k.a. timed writing) are associated with essay exams used by teachers, districts, states, or agencies such as the College Board or ACT to assess students' knowledge of or their ability to write for a certain purpose about a topic or text. In English classes, the quality of the writing should matter as much as the ideas and the content.

4. *Process Paper:* Process papers are those writing assignments, whether long or short, that require students to draft and revise their work in response to feedback from various possible sources. It's not so much a distinct type of writing assignment as it is an instructional approach to teaching writing. Process paper assignments emphasize the quality of the writing as well as the thinking and content.

5. *Research Paper or Report:* Research papers or reports are rare but essential. They prepare students for the longer papers they will write in college. These assignments require students to investigate questions or problems in depth and then anchor their claims and observations in texts, evidence, and findings from research. Such assignments emphasize the quality of the writing as well as the thinking and content; some, however, may place more value on the thinking and content if the assignment is designed to teach the conventions and moves of such writing through shorter forms or what are sometimes called "simulated research" assignments, which are similar to the AP language synthesis essay in that such assignments are often timed and the sources are provided.

6. *Alternative Forms:* Alternative forms share many moves and purposes with traditional academic writing assignments but include such forms as multimedia presentations or other digital forms or hybrids. Some alternative forms focus on the demands of real-world writing, such as résumés, proposals, or business letters. The quality of the writing tends to matter as much as the content, especially if it is for an authentic audience.

Assignments as a Window on Our Work

I was not the only one investigating the writing assignments being created for students. At the college level, around the same time, Dan Melzer (2014) was doing the same, analyzing the 2,101 writing assignments he collected from undergraduate courses across the curriculum. At the middle school level, Santelises and Dabrowski, the authors of a report titled *Checking In: Do Classroom Assignments Reflect Today's Higher Standards?*, were examining over 1,500 middle school assignments from around the country, guided by the idea that "students can rise no higher than the assignments they are given and the instruction they receive" (2015, 3). They went on to explain why assignments are, as I said earlier, the operating system of a school and its curriculum, asserting that these assignments

- ▶ are a clear window into classroom practice;
- ▶ represent what teachers know and understand about the college- and career-ready standards;
- ▶ give insight into the school leader's and/or district's expectations for what and how to teach;
- ▶ reflect what teachers believe students can do independently as a result of their teaching; and
- ▶ show how students interact with the curriculum. (3)

Meanwhile, Arthur Applebee and Judith Langer (2013) were concluding the first major study of middle and high school writing instruction since Applebee's 1981 study, much of which was done through a similar analysis of assignments, as well as observation of teachers in their classrooms. All these studies arrived at more or less the same conclusion: students could write much more than they do, but teachers struggle within the constraints imposed on them by state and district mandates to prepare students for a growing array of exams that limit the types of writing they assign.

My aim in this book is to help us better understand the nature of the academic writing assignments we give our students through the examination of these six different types of assignments we already give in one form or another and to discuss how we might improve what we already do by thinking of them through the principles of design thinking, which are generally broken up into the following stages:

Redesigning Theater's "The Design Thinking Process"

Empathize   Work to fully understand the experience of the user for whom you are designing. Do this through observation, interaction, and immersing yourself in their experiences.

Define	Process and synthesize the findings from your empathy work in order to form a user point of view that you will address with your design.
Ideate	Explore a wide variety of possible solutions through generating a large quantity of diverse possible solutions, allowing you to step beyond the obvious and explore a range of ideas.
Prototype	Transform your ideas into a physical form so that you can experience and interact with them and, in the process, learn and develop more empathy.
Test	Try out high-resolution products and use observations and feedback to refine prototypes, learn more about the user, and refine your original point of view. (Hasso Plattner Institute of Design at Stanford University n.d.)

In recent years, the "users" (the students) for whom we design writing assignments have grown more complex and confusing to us in ways we struggle to understand but need to consider if we—and, more importantly, they—are to be successful. If we focus only on the writing skills we want them to learn through our assignments, ignoring the multiple literacies—academic, cultural, social, and emotional—people such as Alfred Tatum identify as so essential to effective and engaging assignments, we have little hope of assigning work that will have the power to teach and transform students as writers—and people (2005, 35).

The users for whom I design my daily lessons and assignments are profoundly different from those I taught when I arrived at Burlingame High School in the early 1990s. What was then a mostly white student body is now little more than half white, our largest nonwhite group being Latino students, followed by Asian students. For years, I taught AP literature, which became progressively more populated by female students; now, having taught what we call college prep (CP) English for over ten years, I must design my lessons for classes that are as high as 80 percent boys. Yet within my classes, regardless of gender, as many as 80 percent of my students are taking at least one AP class. So the intellectual range, which includes not only these students taking AP classes but also the roughly 20 percent of students with identified learning difficulties, further complicates the design process. This is all to say that knowing and understanding the people for whom we design anything, including writing assignments, is fundamental to the success of whatever we design for them.

The principles of design I discuss throughout this book are grounded in a few assumptions about our work that apply as much to me as they do to all others. First, I assume we share the belief that writing is important, that writing matters, that we know and accept this, even as we struggle to make as much room for it as we would like in our curriculum. Second, I assume that the ideas about design and assignments advanced throughout this book are compatible with those that guide your own instructional approach and philosophy. Whether you think in terms of the number of traits or paragraphs matters not to me here; rather, the framework provided here, which we will revisit throughout the book, is meant to complement your current practice, to merely inform and improve it, as it has my own in the years I have developed it. Third, I intend for these principles to be usable as soon as you sit down to design or refine your next writing assignment, whether it be a short-answer assignment or a major paper. The ideas here require no special training, nor do they seek to displace your current practices. They are, instead, guidelines you can use alongside your existing approach and practice. Finally, the ideas in the Academic Writing Assignment (AWA) Framework discussed throughout are designed to fit whatever grade level or course, whatever ability level or context you might find yourself working in, whether middle or high school, advanced classes or those regular mainstream classes of thirty-five restless seniors such as I teach every day.

Here, then, is the AWA Framework we will return to throughout, which you can apply to your own classes and assignments. Each class and assignment should be

- ▶ *anchored in clear goals linked to specific standards* appropriate to students' age and development, as well as the future exams they will take in class, for the state, or on national assessments;

- ▶ *grounded in texts* that are as engaging as they are demanding in terms of how those texts must be read and used in the writing task;

- ▶ *cognitively demanding* relative to the standards themselves and students' intellectual progress without being overwhelming and thus leaving students feeling defeated;

- ▶ *emotionally and intellectually engaging to all students* to the degree that the assignments give students some measure of choice when it comes to the texts, tasks, and topics they encounter in the context of the writing assignment;

- ▶ *designed to support students* in ways that help them meet the challenges of the writing task while also demonstrating their knowledge and skills legitimately and independently despite such potential obstacles as language or learning difficulties;

► *assessed or evaluated according to criteria and requirements that are clearly stated up front* so students can use them as a guide and know how best to spend their time and energy when writing the assignment; and

► *written and formatted for maximum readability and ease of use* in language that is clear, consistent, concise, and correct, using a layout that makes clear what students need to do and how they need to do it.

Traditional writing assignments have focused on the moves, traits, genres, or rhetorical situations of academic writing, especially those emphasized by various standards documents, which all prize argument above all other writing. As you move through the chapters and the six types of academic writing assignments, you will note that I am offering a different view, one that does not treat each type as a discrete genre; rather, the six types of writing assignments represent the way we really work, the assignments we actually give, and what we can ask students to do within the constraints of time, class size, student needs, and available resources. More often than not, the six different assignments as I describe them here are not stand-alone assignments but tend to prepare students for other larger and often more complex assignments to come. What begins, for example, as a writing-to-learn assignment done in class in students' daybooks often lays the foundation for the short-answer paragraphs they will eventually write about a story we read and about which they'll later write an on-demand paper that draws on those initial short-answer paragraphs, possibly morphing into a process paper they will revise if we have time and cause to treat the on-demand essay as a draft instead of a final destination.

Our writing assignments, of course, must accomplish more than just giving us a way to daisy-chain one to another for a more logical, cohesive sequence. As you will see, in my class reading and writing are inextricably joined, one informing how students will do (and I will teach) the other. Nor are writing assignments ever merely a skill-delivery mechanism in my class; instead, they are carefully designed experiences meant to teach *and* transform, to educate *and* engage. Given the near-universal trend toward collaboration and alignment that PLCs (professional learning communities) and standards have ushered into our departments in the last decade, the writing assignments here also highlight the value and importance of a common language within and across grade levels (and departments, ideally) when it comes to designing writing assignments. In other words, I am motivated as a teacher and, here, as a writer who has worked with schools around the country for the last five years, to address what can seem to be a fragmented curriculum that is frequently undermined by the private practices of some who often seem more interested in leading students up to the inspiration point than getting them to (and beyond) the perspiration point, which is where the learning and growth happen.

Returning to the copy room that morning when I first launched into this inquiry, did the assignments and handouts I waited to run off follow the guidelines I provide here? In ways, in parts, but not fully and not well. Has the aforementioned AWA Framework improved my writing instruction and students' writing performance? Completely. Design thinking and the AWA Framework have taught me to be more intentional, more conscious of the importance of every feature, from the words to the fonts that spell them to the decision to create the assignment for the screen or for paper. It has changed the way I view my role, transforming me from a teacher to a designer not just of documents but of experiences through which students learn how to write better by design.

Reflect on Your Own Practice

Before moving ahead to the first chapter, pause to consider the ideas presented in this introduction and how they apply to your own classes and practice in two areas: the six different types of academic writing assignments and the elements of the Academic Writing Assignment Framework. I suggest you do the following steps in your head, in writing, or as part of a discussion with members of your department or those instructional teams (sometimes called PLCs) to which you belong.

1. Generate a list of all the different writing assignments you have students do in a semester or during a specific unit you just finished or are about to begin. Then, using the six different types of academic writing assignments identified in this chapter as a guide, categorize the different types of writing assignments in your class or unit to determine whether you should consider adding or cutting back on certain types of writing assignments to achieve a more balanced and diverse range of assignments.

2. Examine the assignments on the list you created or a smaller subset of representative assignments in light of the AWA Framework to assess the degree to which these writing assignments include or could be improved to better incorporate the features listed on the framework.

This is, by the way, a good example of what I will refer to throughout the book as a friction point, some feature built into an assignment by design that is intended to draw students' attention to specific elements of the material or provide opportunities for dedicated practice of the skills we want students to learn.

1 Writing to Learn

Practicing Some Mental Moves

> *The way we worked in this class taught us how to think for ourselves. How to evaluate other people's opinions and answers. And that is one of the best ways a person can learn and continue to educate themselves throughout their life.*
>
> —SHANNON MAGUIRE, senior

Writing to Learn (WTL): What It Is and Why We Assign It

Writing to learn (WTL) assignments ask students to *think*, to *use* writing as a tool to help them understand, explore, and discover as they read, write, or discuss different texts and topics. My first experience with WTL was memorable but impossible to imagine in today's classroom: My freshman English teacher asked us to "do a shotgun" in our notebooks about some topic he had assigned us. The obvious question came: "What's a 'shotgun'?" Ken, who insisted we call him by his first name, stood there stirring the honey into his steaming herbal tea (to us, a very exotic thing to drink in 1974) and then said in his whispery voice, "You know, just sort of aim your brain at the page and kinda, you know, blow your brains out on the paper for about fifteen minutes without stopping."

What can I say—it was a different era. We wrote on clipboards; instead of desks, we sat on couches and beanbag chairs. The room had wall-to-wall shag carpet, sort of a burnt orange color only available in the 1970s I expect, that had been rescued from someone's house when it was being remodeled. If you were late, you didn't get detention; instead, you vacuumed the class carpet. Black-light posters covered the walls. It was the closest I came to experiencing the 1960s. I had him as a freshman and a senior; he's the one I would say inspired me to become an English teacher, though that was impossible to imagine at the time.

I mention this brief contact with Ken and the culture of the 1960s because for a good many, the idea of such writing as Ken was assigning—what others have called freewriting or automatic writing—has the taint of the freewheeling days of that era. That is, some hear about this messy sort of writing and think it has no place in the classroom because it lacks rigor and makes limited cognitive demands on students. Yet the truth is that such writing, if designed with specific cognitive processes in mind, creates important opportunities for students to do the extra writing they need to become more fluent but that we do not always have the time to examine or evaluate. This is not to suggest, however, that all such WTL assignments are similar to Ken's shotgun method; nor is such writing divorced from the standards that require students to "write routinely over extended time frames (time for research, reflection, and revision) and shorter time frames (a single sitting or a day or two) for a range of tasks, purposes, and audiences" (Burke 2017b, 70).

These days, I am much more likely to think about the mental moves I want my students to learn to make (and make in order to learn) or the rhetorical moves I want them to master as academic writers. In other words, through WTL assignments, I focus on what I want my students to do *with* their brains, not, as Ken did so long ago, on what they should do *to* their brains. The mental moves typical of most WTL assignments feature words such as *discover, discuss, examine, explore, generate*, and *reflect*. Rose and Kiniry (1997) identified what they called a set of "critical strategies for academic situations," which they argued were central to academic writing and thinking: *defining, summarizing, serializing, classifying, comparing*, and *analyzing*. Others have called out such lists, referring to them as "text structures" that are fundamental to academic writing and of particular importance to helping English learners gain access to the content they must learn and the skills they must develop: *description, sequence, comparison/contrast, cause/effect*, and *problem/solution* (Wilhelm, Smith, and Fredericksen 2012; Olson, Scarcella, and Matuchniak 2015).

Nor do WTL assignments preclude those ways of working that we might compare to the exercises musicians, artists, coders, and others do as part of their apprenticeship into their craft. Often, these WTL assignments serve as a part of the writing process: Students can sketch out a discovery draft of their thinking to figure out what they think about a topic, stepping back from the composing process to jot down some ideas when they are stumped, or reflecting on their process or performance when the paper comes back and they see how they did. Or teachers can use prewriting techniques—listing, outlining, brainstorming, clustering, freewriting, and heuristics—as WTL assignments to help students generate ideas and make connections as they seek to understand and unpack the meaning of a text or topic about which they must write. On other occasions, WTL assignments can help students learn or learn *about* a topic by asking them to think through or try on different ideas by writing their way into such an understanding. Thus, WTL assignments can also serve as writing strategies within the context of the larger writing process for a paper instead of being stand-alone assignments that run the risk of feeling more like busywork in the eyes of our students.

Regardless of the form or means of the writing, the primary aim of WTL assignments is to generate ideas and learn rather than to communicate to any audience other than, for example, the other students with whom one might be engaged in a collaborative online forum or other such situation one might describe as a written conversation. Or, if not to communicate to others through such a written conversation, we design WTL assignments as conversations we want students to enter into with themselves as part of the process of shaping their intellectual and academic identity. In other words, WTL emphasizes acquiring knowledge instead of serving as an assessment meant to demonstrate that students have acquired such knowledge. Because of their more personal or informal nature, WTL assignments can engage students to the extent that they allow for a student's voice and perspective and, during the discovery phase of the writing, downplay the importance of conventions and correctness.

Though WTL assignments are generally not concerned with the style or quality of the writing, they can be if the aim is to improve particular writing skills through such activities as sentence combining or the use of templates to help students emulate more sophisticated writing moves. As WTL assignments tend to serve more as aids to learning, they are typically not used to assess, though a journal, for example, would come in for a grade and some feedback periodically. In order to more fully promote this idea of WTL assignments as focused on learning, I have revised my approach to assessing students' daybooks, which I collect at the end of each of the three grading periods.

Instead of giving students three separate grades on their daybooks, I have them submit their Digital Daybooks (created and maintained in Google Docs) to Turnitin, which serves as a makeshift digital portfolio for all their writing assignments for the year. The grade they receive on their daybook for the first six-week grading period is *replaced* by the grade they receive for their daybook at the end of the second grading period, and the grade they receive for the third grading period counts as the final grade for their Digital Daybook work. The aim of this approach is to reward their improvement in the area of WTL assignments and give them cause to keep working in this area, instead of laboring under the weight of three massive grades they might otherwise get. This approach to assessing the WTL work has been transformative for both students and myself, as it keeps the emphasis where it should be for us all: on learning and improving.

Having conducted an exhaustive study of academic writing in middle and high schools throughout the United States, Applebee and Langer found that students are not writing enough; nor are the tasks they are given making the type of cognitive demands that will prepare them for success in their future endeavors:

> The actual writing that goes on in typical [English language arts] classrooms across the United States remains dominated by tasks in which the teacher does all the composing, and students are left only to fill in missing information, whether copying directly from a teacher's presentation, completing worksheets and chapter summaries, replicating highly formulaic essay structures keyed to high-stakes tests, or writing to "show they know" the particular information the teacher is seeking. Writing as a way to study, learn, and go beyond—as a way to construct knowledge or generate new networks of understanding—is rare. (2013, 27)

It is precisely this idea of "writing as a way to study, learn, and go beyond—as a way to construct knowledge or generate new networks of understanding" that makes WTL assignments an important way to promote a more interactive, engaged approach to teaching writing that does not increase our paper load. Such assignments make room for serious and intentional academic writing in the classroom without displacing the other types of writing assignments that form more of the core of the academic writing curriculum. If we make the effort to design these WTL assignments well enough, they can also provide the support so many students, especially students who struggle with writing, require if they are to succeed on those core academic writing assignments addressed in other chapters here.

Before moving on, I think it's a good idea to provide a few general examples of the range of WTL assignments from my class to clarify what such assignments can look like. Whether teaching freshmen or seniors, college prep or advanced classes, I regularly design and assign WTL tasks that ask students to

- ▶ reflect on their progress, process, and performance;
- ▶ practice crafting different types of sentence structures about texts we are reading as a way of embedding writing instruction within the context of reading;
- ▶ engage in written or collaborative conversations online with peers in response to specified topics, texts, or tasks;
- ▶ use structured note-taking and other sorts of tools and techniques to improve understanding of texts and topics;

- ▶ demonstrate their understanding through informal assignments such as exit tickets; or
- ▶ write in their notebooks for a wide range of purposes related to what we are reading, discussing, or learning.

Though it may seem to be the sort of assignment my high school teacher would have had us do a shotgun about, the following example offers one quick glimpse into WTL assignments in my class. Each year I take seniors out to the football field, directing them to spread out along the yard line that corresponds with their age at that time. They sit on the seventeen- and eighteen-yard lines, while I trudge a bit farther each year to sit on the line that corresponds with my own age. In their notebooks, students are to write about what it feels like to be the age they are, a topic that might seem too soft, too personal, to some; yet they are engaging in this writing activity not just because it is a good thing for them to think about in October of their senior year but also because when we return to the classroom after about twenty minutes, we will use their writing to launch our reading and initial discussion of *Into the Wild*, by Jon Krakauer (1996), which we will begin reading that day. As depicted in Figures 1–1a and 1–1b, here are two sample responses from different types of students.

FIGURE 1–1b Students find the use of physical environments such as the football field engaging and useful prompts to their thinking, in this case, about what life is like when you are seventeen or eighteen.

FIGURE 1–1a Chi Le Tang forgot his daybook so wrote his daybook entry that day on his phone.

Nick wrote:

Reflection on the Field

It is still unbelievable to me that I am now a senior in high school. As a little kid, I thought I'd be a lot more mature and organized about the path I would want to take for my post high-school life. But here I am today, not even sure what my path is. My life is full of uncertainties at the moment and my maturity is being tested more on how I handle these uncertainties rather than executing maturity by following a path. As I fill out my college applications, I know that the way I handle these pressures that accompany it (choosing my college, major, what to write my college app essays about, etc.) will reflect how I will handle similar situations down the line. I will learn from this. In my future, though, I do have an overall goal: to live a stable yet <u>fulfilling</u> life.

Hanna wrote:

I wish that in my life, school-wise, that I would have succeeded at my greatest potential, because I will admit, I didn't. Currently, I have a 4.0, the best I've ever had in school, and I could have at least gotten close to those grades sixth through sophomore year, because last year is when I started to care. But instead, I focused more on other things. And now I am being punished for what I thought was a good idea at the time. And a college that should be my safety school is now my "reach school" and now I may not be getting into my dream school. Looking back, I would have loved to tell myself to do better because now I am stuck in a position I don't want to be in, where I'm now probably going to be stuck at College of San Mateo, which might not be such a bad thing any more.

In his study of over 2,000 college writing assignments across all disciplines, Melzer found that the short-answer exam dominated; however, he noted that WTL assignments "effectively address" the demands of such short-answer assignments (2014, 16). Additionally, Melzer found that 21 percent of those courses that emphasized writing across the curriculum asked students to engage in the sort of self-reflective, metacognitive writing that you see my students doing in the previous examples and in those examples that appear throughout the rest of this chapter. The sort of writing this chapter examines challenges the practices of some and validates that of others, but the value of it is clear if the tasks are intentional and carefully designed. David Russell said of WTL, "From very early in the history of mass education, writing was primarily thought of as a way to examine students, not to teach them, as a means of demonstrating knowledge rather than acquiring it" (1991, 6). The ideas and examples that follow challenge such traditional perspectives and practices.

What Students Say and How They Struggle with WTL Assignments

Student perspectives on WTL assignments vary. Many appreciate the lack of immediate pressure typical of most WTL assignments; others, however, see such assignments as optional, trivial, even irrelevant insofar as they often go ungraded or serve as a means rather than an end in themselves. Thus when we design WTL assignments and activities, we should be mindful of these attitudes. In most cases, providing a clear and legitimate rationale for what we are trying to accomplish through any WTL assignment will suffice. In other words, students want to know the problem for which a WTL activity is the solution. Or, as some have said, students do not care about the *what* or the *how* until they know the *why*.

As with many other types of writing, WTL assignments come with an array of potential obstacles we must consider when designing them. Students speak of not understanding the task or the directions themselves, which are more likely to be spelled out orally and on the fly because of the less formal and less structured quality of many WTL tasks. Other students struggle to understand not the task but rather the text or topic a WTL assignment is intended to help them better comprehend.

Also, students' lack of engagement or motivation can easily undermine the success of some WTL assignments. In such situations, students respond much as Bartleby did to assignments given by his boss: "I'd prefer not to." One of the greatest struggles students experience derives from the same problem WTL assignments are designed to address: the challenge of generating ideas, language, and questions. Each student's performance is something like an old-fashioned hand pump: some people pump once and the water flows; others need to pump a few times to prime the pump before the water will come; still others pump in earnest only to find that nothing comes from their effort and so these students give up, believing they have nothing to say or lack the ability to say it.

Because the design thinking approach suggests we always begin by empathizing with those for whom we are designing anything, I try to gather as much information as I can about students' attitudes toward writing early in the year and monitor their responses through regular self-reflections about their progress as we go. My survey of over one hundred seniors regarding their past experience with WTL assignments and activities revealed useful insights, as the participants were a representative group. Of all the different WTL tasks listed, my students found "freewriting or brainstorming to generate ideas and questions" the most helpful (90 percent), followed closely by outlining (83 percent) and note-taking (78 percent) and summarizing or paraphrasing key concepts from lectures, assigned reading, and videos (75 percent). A sizeable group did not find helpful such techniques as having students generate test questions (53 percent) or responding to writing prompts about what students read or learned about in a lecture (31 percent). Perhaps most surprising of the results is that nearly half (47 percent) said they had never been asked by a previous teacher to use a journal or notebook for reflection, problem solving, or recordkeeping.

Designing WTL assignments and activities presents unique challenges when compared with most of the other types of writing assignments discussed in this book. WTL assignments remind me of the workouts my tennis coach planned for me so I would be ready to play the actual matches, for which everything else was preparation. WTL feels more like practice than performance, more like a workout than the game we are preparing our students to play. Thus, when we design WTL assignments, we should remain clear about their purpose and place in the larger scheme of our curriculum, making sure as we create them that these assignments anticipate and address those areas where students are likely to struggle. If we fail to empathize with students when constructing WTL tasks, the assignments themselves will fail to engage and, as a result, educate as intended. In this sense, we realize that we are not designing assignments or activities but, rather, experiences that are intended to challenge our students at every turn so that they can improve regardless of their current level of performance.

The Forms and Features of WTL Assignments

As with the other types of writing assignments I discussed in the Introduction, WTL tasks function less as stand-alone assignments and more as the work an apprentice might do in the course of learning a craft—in this case, reading, writing, discussing, and thinking. Applebee and Langer, in their study of academic writing, recommend that teachers emphasize "the processes of apprenticeship and immersion in disciplinary activity," which they argue requires students to engage in an "apprenticeship in the text practices of the discipline over time" (2013, 183). Through WTL assignments, students develop academic literacy through what Applebee and Langer call these "essential disciplinary experiences" (183).

Before we examine specific forms and features of WTL assignments, let us review some of the aspects of these assignments in general. Such assignments tend to be short, informal, often improvised writing activities, which are more likely to be checked and scanned than graded and read. Their primary aim is to nurture critical thinking and disciplinary learning. According to Toby Fulwiler and Art Young, "the primary function [of writing to learn] is not to communicate, but to order and represent [the] experience" of our own understanding by using writing as "a tool for discovering, for shaping meaning, and for reaching understanding" (1982, 4). Indeed, writing to think is a constant thread in discussions of WTL, bringing to light what some see as the fundamental dichotomy we face when designing such writing assignments:

> As teachers we can choose between (a) sentencing students to thoughtless mechanical operations and (b) facilitating their ability to think. If students' readiness for more involved thought processes is bypassed in favor of jamming more facts and figures into their heads, they will stagnate at the lower levels of thinking. But if students are encouraged to try a variety of thought processes in classes, they can, regardless of their ages, develop considerable mental power. Writing is one of the most effective ways to develop thinking. (Forsman 1985, 162)

When discussing the different forms of WTL assignments and activities, we should distinguish between the writing and where, why, and how to do it. Over the course of a year, students in my classes engage in WTL work using composition books, sticky notes, poster paper, idea boards (large clipboards painted with IdeaPaint dry-erase paint, which turns them into portable whiteboards around which students can gather), index cards, margins (for annotations), and various computer applications, especially Google Docs. Such writing takes place in different configurations: individually, collaboratively, often both, with students beginning on their own and then merging their ideas into one document through collaborative discussion about the assigned text or topic (see Figures 1–2 through 1–7).

FIGURE 1–2 WTL assignments work well in all sizes and on all surfaces. Here, two boys summarize and prepare to present their ideas about a section of Carol Dweck's book *Mindset*.

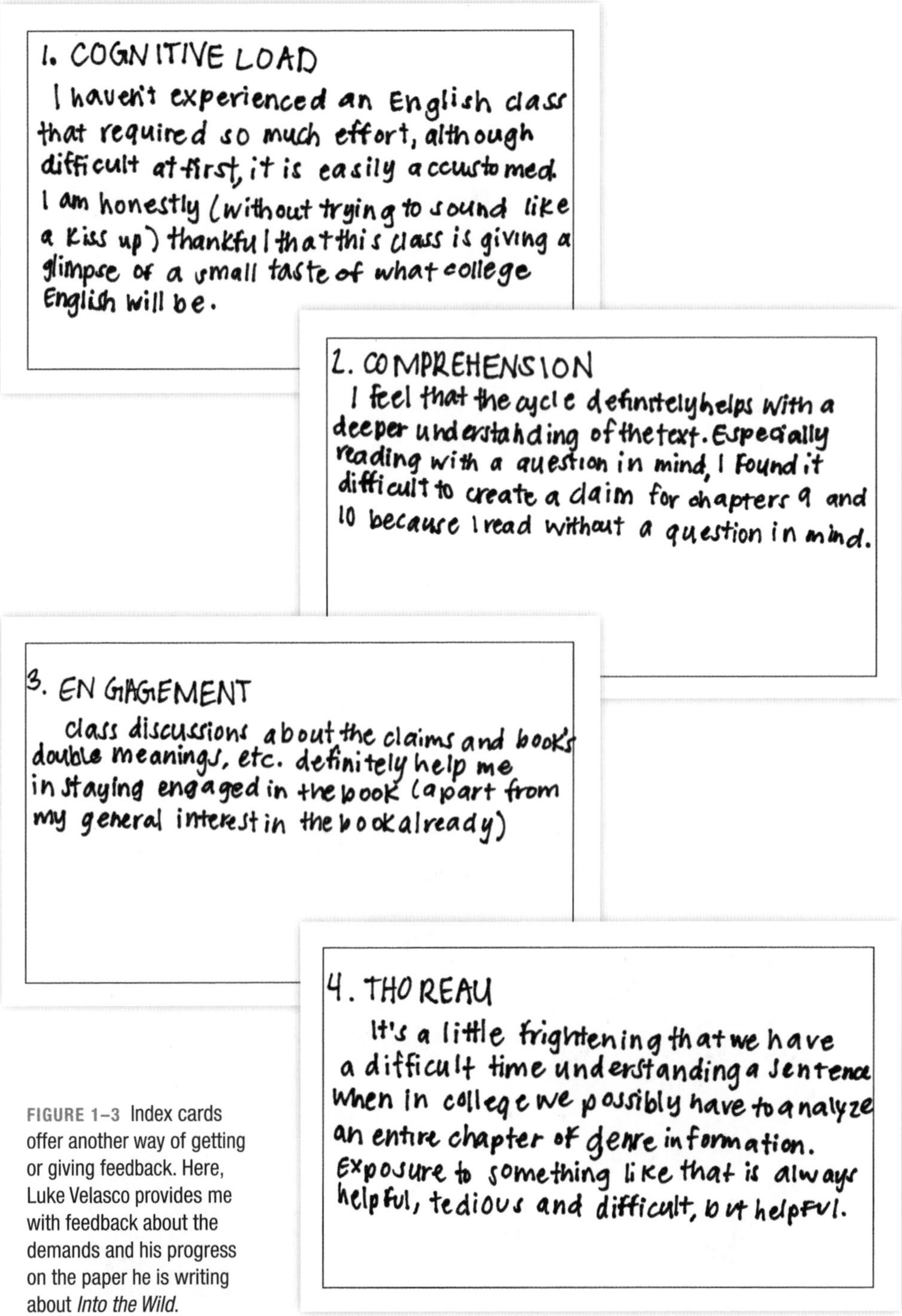

1. COGNITIVE LOAD

I haven't experienced an English class that required so much effort, although difficult at first, it is easily accustomed. I am honestly (without trying to sound like a kiss up) thankful that this class is giving a glimpse of a small taste of what college English will be.

2. COMPREHENSION

I feel that the cycle definitely helps with a deeper understanding of the text. Especially reading with a question in mind, I found it difficult to create a claim for chapters 9 and 10 because I read without a question in mind.

3. ENGAGEMENT

class discussions about the claims and book's double meanings, etc. definitely help me in staying engaged in the book (apart from my general interest in the book already)

4. THOREAU

It's a little frightening that we have a difficult time understanding a sentence when in college we possibly have to analyze an entire chapter of genre information. Exposure to something like that is always helpful, tedious and difficult, but helpful.

FIGURE 1–3 Index cards offer another way of getting or giving feedback. Here, Luke Velasco provides me with feedback about the demands and his progress on the paper he is writing about *Into the Wild*.

While they appear to be the same, the labrynth and maze differ in many ways that give us some insight into our own personality and world view. The labrynth's path is much longer with only one path that will never fail to lead an individual to the final destination. However, the maze is remotely shorter with opportunities woven throughout to make errors. One might say those who prefer the labyrinth favor support more than those who like the maze. Even if it may take longer, they'd rather know they're right. Whereas people who prefer the maze are more comfortable with making mistakes and will risk that if it means there's a shorter amount of time/distance to the "finish line".

8/18/16

Of all the demands of school, english/writing is probably one of my least favorite subjects. I enjoy thinking strategically and logically about complex tasks and topics, however, it is difficult for me to take those thoughts and transition them on to paper. I always understand what I'm trying to say and it makes sense to me, but other people always have some confusion when they read it themself. I tend to forget to include key ideas, thoughts or explanations when writing that lead to that grey area for other people which is what I need to work on the most.

8/23/16

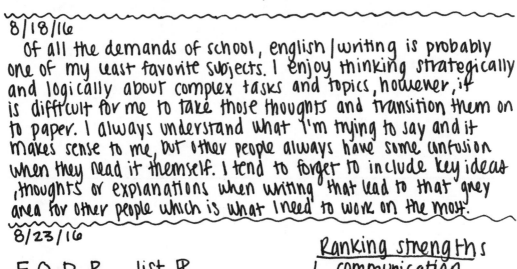

F O D P   list P
Focus Organization Development Purpose   1 FOCUS line
                    2 ↗ ↗ ↗
                    2   Dev./org.
                    2
                    2
                    2

Ranking strengths
1. communication
2. relator
3. self-assurance
4. competition
5. belief

FIGURE 1–4 The daybook offers Kyra a space to reflect, respond, capture notes, and practice her analytical writing.

Overview

This tool is designed to help you do some initial thinking about your subject as you prepare to begin your project. The idea for right now is to come up with as many ideas as possible, then see which idea interests you the most and seems the most viable topic. The first tool generates ideas; the second one helps you narrow, refine, and begin to develop.

Directions:

1. Write your subject (e.g., food) in the center of the target on top.

2. In first ring ("categories"), put symbols, single words, or very short phrases that identify the smaller slices we can use to consider the topic and generate ideas for the one you finally choose.

3. In the outer ring ("description"), jot down a very brief note that explains something about this category, its importance, and its relevance.

4. Choose one slice from the top organizer and write that in the middle of the tool on the bottom. This should be written as a phrase (e.g. "the effect of technology on relationships").

5. In the four "Aspect" boxes, generate four aspects or sides of the topic, then fill each box in with ideas, questions, or examples.

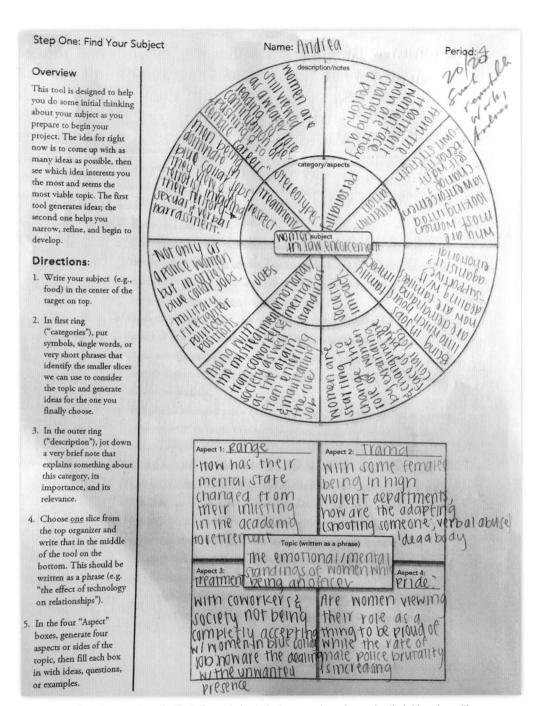

FIGURE 1–5 Organizers such as the Topic Target help students generate and organize their ideas by writing about them in more structured ways. Here, Andrea is beginning the process of clarifying and refining her topic for the Expert Project.

"The Secret Powers of Time"

They say / I say
[Notes]

They say...	I say...
Time Perspective	
• Past / Present / Future oriented ["4 time zones"]	I agree, especially with it being categorized into two: futuristic or past/ present although there is room for change
• Past can be + or − (regrets)	
• To be future oriented you need to have trust, make sacrifices	
• In the North, people are more future oriented, in the South people are more past/present ex: Italy (½)	I agree. I think there are several factors that apply to people's perspective of time individually, like said: cultures, where you live, who you live with... what you like to do in your free time, who your friends are...
Perception of Time	
• People of different cultures have different 'pace of life' or sense of duration	
• "school is designed to transform present to future oriented"	
• technology digitally rewires the brain → fundamental change	→ like the family meal example, kids are more likely to be futuristic because of their family values. Alot of things can factor in each individuals sense of duration, and/or perception of time.
• puzzles can be solved by simply understanding yours/others time perspective	

FIGURE 1–6 In this WTL example, a student is taking notes on a TED Talk by Philip Zimbardo using ideas from the they say/I say format, which will later help her write a paragraph in which she summarizes and responds to Zimbardo's ideas.

FIGURE 1–7 It is easy to start using the laptops for everything, but much research suggests a more interactive approach that disrupts students' more passive watching improves engagement and comprehension. Here we see Nuha and Ethan taking notes on a short documentary related to Rebecca Skloot's *The Immortal Life of Henrietta Lacks* (2010) as we begin reading that book.

As for the forms of WTL assignments themselves, I would group them according to not just form but also format and function within the larger curriculum. With this in mind, we should design WTL experiences that use writing to improve students' ability to do the following:

▶ *Read a range of print and visual texts* using the following techniques:

• Writing on (annotating) or about (responding, interpreting, analyzing) texts for specified academic purposes in response to questions, prompts, or topics the teacher provides or students develop themselves. You can have students first write a response to a text and then annotate their own response with added comments, a technique commonly used by Michel de Montaigne, who would return to his own writing and continue to add new ideas and insights in the margins.

Summary
Notes

Rhetorical
Précis Notes

• Summarizing, paraphrasing, or writing a rhetorical précis using the Summary Notes or Rhetorical Précis Notes template and model—or just a basic index card quickly distributed and easily collected and checked. (See Figure 1–8.)

> *French and Raven's Six Forms of Power*
>
> In summary, everyone has power that is sourced from six different bases of power. Each basis defines how a person can use their power in any setting. As the article states, the most effective leaders adapt referent and expert powers. This gives them the ability to develop leadership qualities and inflict positive influences on your employees. In juxtaposition, coercive power can be seen as negative because it conditions people into submission through the ability to punish one for their behavior. All have different powers, what's yours?

FIGURE 1–8 While Jonathan could as easily have written this summary of French and Raven's power model in his daybook, the index card offers the advantage of more accountability if used as a sort of exit ticket.

▶ *Write about different texts and topics* by doing the following:

- Providing students with sentence frames or templates that model more sophisticated moves students can use to write about complex ideas and texts.

Academic Writing Moves: Patterns and Purposes Overview

- Composing a well-organized paragraph with effective transitions and other features appropriate to the purpose through collaborative discussion with students as you facilitate the discussion while capturing their initial ideas, which they then complete on their own in response to the specified text, as in this example from our work with *The Immortal Life of Henrietta Lacks*:

> **In Your Notebook:** Write a summary of the epigraph by Elie Wiesel, the prologue, and the first five chapters that uses the following structure/moves:
>
> > Rebecca Skloot *begins* her book with an epigraph by Elie Wiesel that declares . . . In the prologue that follows, Skloot *describes* . . . Having *established* the context for the story that follows, Skloot *opens* with . . . Instead of settling into the story of Henrietta's illness, however, Skloot *shifts* her focus to . . . Following the previous chapter's detour into Henrietta's past, Rebecca Skloot *recounts* . . . In the following chapter, titled "The Birth of Hela," we *learn* . . . Meanwhile, as Skloot *makes clear* in Chapter 5, . . .

- Creating a structured note-taking tool designed to guide students' thinking as they read and write in response to a text. Figure 1–9 provides one example of a tool my students used to write about the challenges Justice Sonya Sotomayor

THE LESSONS OF STRUGGLE AND FAILURE FROM JUSTICE SOTOMAYOR'S MEMOIR

Directions: In your groups, add to this table examples of when Sotomayor struggled or failed and then complete the rest of the row with examples, details, and explanations of what happened, what it means, and why it matters. Be prepared to discuss your contributions. Each group should identify itself at the beginning of each row it fills in. Groups may fill in more than one row but may not duplicate existing content unless your group has a different angle or perspective on it.

Group	WHEN did Sotomayor fail/struggle?	WHY did Sotomayor fail/struggle?	HOW did Sotomayor respond?	WHAT did Sotomayor learn from it?	SO? How did it shape her character?
Jack Gunnar Isabelle Rachel	When she got a C on her paper.	This was a failure to Sotomayor because of her high personal standards and her desire to prove herself given her background.	She took failure as a challenge to improve herself and her education. She found out that she needed to improve her grammar in order to fix her writing, so she spent her time studying.	She obviously learned grammar and vocabulary skills, but more importantly she learned how to cope with and confront failure.	She became able to write her senior thesis at the end of her college career and later went on to be a Supreme Court Justice.
Jack Caitlyn Anmol	When she realized her English wasn't as correct in her writing, and received a C on an assignment.	She felt like an outcast and therefore doubted her own abilities. She wasn't used to receiving low grades.	She bought grammar and vocab books/sets to practice correct sentence structure and to correct her improper English.	She learned to take responsibility when she struggled while keeping a positive attitude.	Sotomayor learned she was capable of much more than she thought and her confidence increased majorly.
Niko Justin Paul Camryn Kenneally	Sotomayor felt like she had failed when she was getting poor English grades.	She faced struggle because English was a second language and her inability to properly dissect the language made her feel like she was not good enough to excel.	Sotomayor responded by meeting with her teacher to see what she was doing wrong and then spending extra time to learn and improve her English skills through grammar/vocabulary books and novels.	Sotomayor learned that she could overcome the obstacles caused by her background and that with an open mindset she could improve upon her skills. As well as the ability to love learning.	Sotomayor developed a stronger character by using her early setbacks as an opportunity to develop an even stronger foundation and reach new levels of success.
Josh Hannah Brennan	Sotomayor struggled during her transition from a poorer environment to the wealthy Princeton status.	When she was at a house party, she listened in on people talking about a wedding and buying something off of a bridal registry. . . . She thought, "What the hell is a bridal registry . . . Were people here so rich they could afford a wedding without gifts of cash?" (72). She had a difficult time during that transition between rich and poor.	Sotomayor responded by spending time in the library whenever she felt out of place.	Sotomayor learned that she would have to soon adapt to her surroundings and the people if she wanted to assimilate.	It shaped her character because she transitioned into a growth mindset through the various experiences.
Bernard Chris Charmaine	Sotomayor struggled her first year of college because of how misplaced she felt at Princeton.	The new environment was uncomfortable for Sotomayor, making her feel like an outcast. Sotomayor also felt intimidated by how advanced her peers were academically.	Sotomayor overcame her homesickness and loneliness by spending time at the Firestone Library as well as dedicating time to catch up with her fellow classmates.	Sotomayor learned that she needed to work hard to make friends or set up activities that helped her feel less like an outcast.	This shaped her to be more of an outgoing person with the understanding of people's outlooks and different cultures.

FIGURE 1–9 The benefit of designing such structured note-taking tools as I did here is that we can target those moves we want them to make as readers, writers, and thinkers.

© 2019 by Jim Burke from *The Six Academic Writing Assignments*. Portsmouth, NH: Heinemann.

faced and overcame during her first year of college. I created the handout in Google Docs and then shared out the link to all students with editing privileges so all could contribute to the same document, which they could keep and use for the subsequent essay about Dweck's mindset theory and how it applies to different readings, such as Sotomayor's.

- Giving students specific sentence frames to help them learn the conventions of academic writing, such as this example, which asks students to first watch and then write about a TED Talk, in this case one given by Philip Zimbardo, which we viewed in the context of reading the novel *Siddhartha*, by Hermann Hesse:

> **Directions:** Watch the Philip Zimbardo TED Talk titled "The Secret Powers of Time," keeping in mind your own views about time as well as Siddhartha's. After you watch it, use the following sentence templates to write about Zimbardo's ideas:
>
> 1. In his "time perspective" theory, Stanford psychologist Philip Zimbardo argues that . . .
>
> 2. In other words, Zimbardo means . . .
>
> 3. His theory, which emphasizes how our perspective on time affects _____, has important implications for _____ because it suggests that . . .

▶ *Discuss challenging texts* by asking students to:

- Take structured notes using specific techniques (see Online Resources for Cornell Notes, Q Notes, Listener's Notes) while reading, viewing, or listening to the assigned text(s); then use those notes to guide small-group or full-class discussions about the text.

Cornell Notes

- Jot down keywords, connections, or passages from the text on sticky notes students then stick on the whiteboard; then, each student chooses someone else's sticky note and writes about that to prepare for the subsequent discussion. The examples provided in Figure 1–10 come from my AP literature class when we were reading Dostoyevsky's *Crime and Punishment*.

Q Notes

Listener's Notes

- Generate questions about the text or subject being discussed, which they can post to a class Google Doc (or via some other app that allows the class or everyone in a group to post his or her own thoughts and respond to others' ideas); then, students choose one question and write about it as directed within the app or in their discussion group before sharing and responding to others' comments.

Self Hatred

- constant questioning of ones actions
- unsure of yourself / your actions
- what encourages this?

Interconflict

- for a majority of the beginning of the novel, Raskolnikov fights between whether he should or should not kill Alyona.
- many things change his mind before he ends up killing her.

Attitude towards Society

- Rasolnikov always seems condescending toward people wearing rags - but he too wears them (more & less)
- He seems happy/relieved after he's called into Police (& its not about murder) even though nessesarnen

VALUE (of morals, or money)

Raskolnikov's main motivation for murder is for money since he is so poor, yet he gives it away so easily to those in need. How much does he really value money?

Mental Stages

Dostoevsky constantly refers to what Raskolnikov thinks and how his thoughts and actions are not regulated.
- his inevitable act of murder is haunting him and driving him crazy.

COURAGE / BRAVERY

is it an act of courage to murder Alyona or one of cowardice?

Expectations
- is Rosko responsible for his sister and mother.
- is he expected to live up to his father?
- what is he expecting from society
  - why does he expect society to respect him
- He expects a life, but isn't trying to achieve it honestly
  - He's setting himself for disappointment

FIGURE 1–10 Sticky notes create opportunities for more interactive ways of generating ideas that do not rely on or take the time certain apps might. In this example, it is the questions on the sticky notes and the way we use them to foster conversations about the texts that make the difference.

▶ *Think critically about what they read and learn* by having them:

- Write about the text or topic from a perspective other than their own, explaining the reasoning and implications of their position. This could mean having students write in the voice and from the perspective of a character in the text, from history, or in modern times; it could also mean writing about the question, text, or topic *as if you agreed* with the source (called the Believing Game) or *as if you disagreed* with the source (called the Doubting Game).

- Translate quantitative data into a written form (a data table into a paragraph) that explains what the data say, what they mean, and why that matters using the Says–Means–Matters tool (see Figure 1–11).

- Examine some key aspect of the subject or text by creating a visual representation, symbol, or metaphor on their own or in groups; then, have students write up and present to the class their idea, as students in Figure 1– 12 did when creating a visual explanation of the contribution Henrietta Lacks made to modern science and society.

Here is Nina's explanation, taken from her notebook, of their visual explanation in Figure 1-12:

In Part 1, Skloot details Henrietta's life until her death, which also led to the start of HeLa's impact on the world. We drew a bomb because the cancer cells were like ticking time bombs in HeLa, something that, in time, would eventually go off. We put the events leading to her death on the fuse, as everything that happened up to her death, before she died, which was just before the bomb. Inside the bomb, we put things that hit the world like explosions, changing the world as we knew it with the discovery of the polio vaccine and creation of HeLa factories. We put all events related to Henrietta in green because of the happiness and emotions she stirred in others around her, and we put other events in orange to make it seem like they were lighting the fuse to the explosion of the HeLa cells on the world. The lighting of the fuse was when she was born because that's when it all started. It's her birth that started everything. I think we also did it because it wasn't one that stood out, like it was [a] normal looking bomb but they both exploded into the world, changing it greatly forever and for the better. We wrote things that happened after Henrietta died in gold to symbolize her value to the world, that her cells were gold mines and extremely desirable and possibly unattainable for some people.

AUTHOR NOTES: SAYS—MEANS—MATTERS

Name: _____   Period: _____

Text/Author: _____

Directions: Take notes and write down your thoughts as directed while reading your assigned text on your own and with your reading group. Take these notes on a separate sheet of paper, though you may begin by using this sheet if you wish.

1. **Title Thoughts:** Jot down some thoughts, questions, or associations in response to the title.

2. **Purpose Question (PQ):** Generate a PQ in response to the title and/or the first paragraph.

3. **Notes:** Look for and examine key ideas and quotations as you read, using the format and templates below as a guide.

WHAT THE AUTHOR SAYS	WHAT THE AUTHOR MEANS	WHY IT MATTERS
Identify and write down the direct quotation and page number of a passage that is important to the author's main point.	Translate the author's words into your own by paraphrasing his or her words and explaining why you think that is what the author means.	Explain the meaning and importance of the author's words and the reasoning behind your assertion about their importance.
At one point, X observes that . . . X describes _____ as . . . X seems to think _____ since she writes . . .	X means, in other words, that . . . What X is saying is that . . . Here, X implies that . . .	This observation by X that _____ is important because it suggests/shows that . . . When X says that _____, X is not saying _____ but is, instead, insisting that . . . X wants us to understand, when he says this, that _____ matters because it shows . . .
Sample Describing the kids he grew up with, Rose calls them "a funny mix brought together by geography and parental desire" (1).	**Sample** Their parents, in other words, moved to this part of town hoping to find a better life for themselves and, most importantly, their children.	**Sample** Those parents, believing that "hope had set up shop in the west end of the county," however, could only afford to live on the border of the world they hoped to enter by getting their children a better education.

FIGURE 1–11 Author's Notes: Says–Means–Matters tool

FIGURE 1–12 Infographics and other such visual explanations offer important opportunities to generate ideas and make connections that can be adapted into more developed writing assignments later, as Nina Hsu and her group demonstrate.

▶ *Assess their own understanding about the topics and texts they read and investigate* by asking students to

- Transform an article or TED Talk into a three-slide PowerPoint that emphasizes writing with clarity and concision. You can, for example, tell them to create three slides with three bullets per slide organized under headers that identify the three key ideas of the topic or text.

- Write a one-minute or five-minute essay at the end of the period that they turn in on their way out as a variation on the exit ticket strategy.

- Summarize on one side of the page or index card what they learned from an article, video, or discussion; then, on the other side, have them write what they think and what they think is most important—and why.

▶ *Examine their progress, performance, or process* by asking them to

- Reflect on their performance on a completed or revised paper, focusing on what strategies they used and how these helped them write the paper.

- Describe their progress in a specific area such as writing, including in their reflection any reasons and evidence that support their claims about their progress in that area; also, they should include in their discussion what caused this progress so they can be more aware of it and intentional in the future on such assignments.

- Make the case for the grade their paper should get, providing evidence and reasoning to support their position. Or ask them to declare what grade they would want on the paper they are about to begin writing and outline what they must do to achieve that result, an instructional strategy Hattie found had the greatest effect size of all the measures he examined in his exhaustive meta-analysis (2009, 43).

If you want to simplify much of what I have said here, simply think: BDA (before, during, after). That is, when designing WTL assignments, pause at each of these three stages in your own process and consider what you might ask students to write before, during, and after anything else you might have them do. I am not saying you should always have students write at each one of those points; rather, use BDA as one might a flowchart, to remind you that we always have choices about what to have students do in our classes. When it comes to designing WTL assignments, we should be guided by one question: *What is the problem for which having them write at this point (or about this topic, or in this way) is the solution?* If the WTL work is not intentional—if it does not challenge or engage students—it is unlikely to make the difference we hoped the task would and we should change the assignment or not require it.

These assignments and those examined in depth in the section that follows all conform to, or are at least designed to satisfy, the Academic Writing Assignment Framework outlined before and included here in an abbreviated version, which suggests that all academic writing assignments be:

- ▶ anchored in clear goals linked to specific standards;
- ▶ grounded in texts that are engaging and demanding;
- ▶ cognitively demanding;
- ▶ emotionally and intellectually engaging to all students;
- ▶ designed to support students;
- ▶ assessed or evaluated according to criteria and requirements that are clearly stated; and
- ▶ written and formatted for maximum readability and ease of use.

Keep these guidelines in mind as you read through the next section, where I dive into a few specific case studies from my class to show you what all this looks like in action.

Classroom Connection: What WTL Looks Like in My Class

Students write just about every day in my class in one form or another, mostly for academic purposes. Here, I would like to examine two different types of WTL assignments that represent different approaches—one that is structured and one that is more improvised but always consistent with the principles of academic apprenticeship and the Academic Writing Assignment Framework.

The Digital Daybook

Heading into the homestretch of the spring semester, I faced the daunting prospect of 100 seniors who could sense if not see the finish line of high school. Some of them were gripped by the upcoming prospect of AP exams and thus felt little should be asked of them at that point in the year. Those who were not taking AP exams felt that almost nothing should be expected of them. On top of all these factors, I had one hundred Expert Project papers (see Chapter 5 for more on this major research assignment) to read. These papers averaged around ten pages and demanded a lot of time and attention as they were the culmination of a yearlong project. And, the last book of the year awaited us: *1984*.

How to do all this—read *1984* in a way that would engage one hundred seniors as spring began to dance outside the windows and still keep working to improve my students' abilities as academic writers, since their Expert Project papers, though accomplished, showed they clearly had more to learn when it came to academic writing? I decided to have them create a Google Doc we would call the Digital Daybook. It would be a place where they could work on writing as Don Murray did in his own daybook, which he described as a place where he was often "playing with writing" in order to "keep [his] writing muscles in condition" (2005, 56). Murray's daybook was a space in which he listed, generated, captured, and generally "thought and rethought, planned and researched, drafted and redrafted" his ideas (56). It was not, as Murray says emphatically, a journal or a diary; for my students, it was, as Murray says it can be, written on a computer in a file titled "Daybook."

In my class, we read *1984* (1949) as an inquiry into power, a topic seniors are much more interested in at this point in their lives than the more abstract idea of a dystopian future dreamed up by Orwell. Their Digital Daybook worked like this most days: Upon entering class, they fetched their assigned Chromebooks from the cart, opened up the Daily Record (see Figure 1–13), and followed the directions spelled out there.

Thursday, August 24,

The Daily Record • Mr. Burke • Senior English

FOCUS

Mind-set and ideas related to it and applied to "Personal Prologue" and self; also, pivotal moments that teach us, shape us (*educere*).

OBJECTIVES

Transfer ideas from diagram to writing.
Introduce and begin reading Dweck article and discussing its place in the unit.

NOTES & REMINDERS

Watch BTV News 4°
Buddies Day Friday

ACT 1: THE DIGITAL DAYBOOK

1. Digital Daybook (insert page break + header 1 "Pivotal Moments"
+ check TOC).
2. Use your phone to snap a photo of your completed character arc
from last night.
3. Insert the photo into your Digital Daybook entry for today: Crop and use
text wrap as needed (as I did for the image to the right).
4. Use the character arc as a guide to write an explanation of what it says/
shows and means. The lines under "Beginning" and "End" represent the
words you might use to describe yourself at each stage. When writing, pay attention to your verbs and transitions, keeping in
mind my own essay as a model to guide you. Also, keep asking yourself what each pivotal moment means and why it matters.

ACT 2: DISCUSS DAMON'S "PATHS TO PURPOSE" (4 + 1 TYPES)

1. In his study of adolescent purpose, Damon found four types—purposeful, dreamers, dabblers, and disengaged—as well as
a fifth, the "dangerously disturbed," who are exemplified by the two Columbine killers. Which one do you think best charac-
terizes the author of "The Personal Prologue"? Why? Which one best describes *you* at this point in your life? Why?

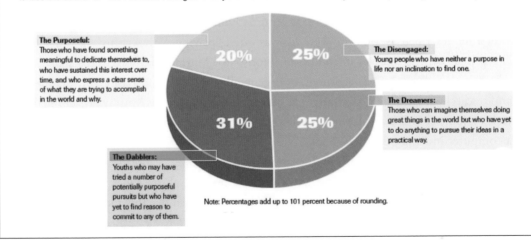

FIGURE 1–13 The Daily Record, which is the lesson plan I write up each day, is a Google Doc I display via students' laptop
screens and the LCD screen up front. The template of the Daily Record document itself serves to nudge me, by design, to be
more structured and clear when writing up my lesson plan since my students and I are both users of the document. (*continues*)

The Daily Record • Mr. Burke • Senior English

ACT 3: "THE MINDSETS" (DWECK)

1. Discuss the idea of mindsets as you imagine it: what it is, implies.

2. Read Dweck's "Mindset" for Friday and come in prepared to discuss and write about the questions at the end. That is, read the excerpt (from her book) straight through (pages 54–65), focusing on what a mindset is and means; we will discuss and write about it in class tomorrow. This excerpt is important to all the other readings as it will serve as the basis for the paper you will write.

SO WHAT?

Growth mindset is central to your ability to learn and improve.

If you do not believe you can learn or improve, you will think: Why bother?

HOMEWORK

Finish "The Mindsets" in *Uncharted Territory*.

Bring book to class on Friday.

Binder: You need a one- to two-inch three-ring binder and five dividers and paper. I have a number of binders for those who would like to take one.

WHAT TO REMEMBER

Mindset

Bring book

Binder with paper

WHAT WAS ON THE BOARD

Not sure if I can promise to always remember to do this, but I thought I would try to snap a quick picture of whatever was on the board and tack it on here at the end. Mostly, the board contents only make sense in the context of the class period when I am scribbling them on there, but who knows—could prompt us to remember things.

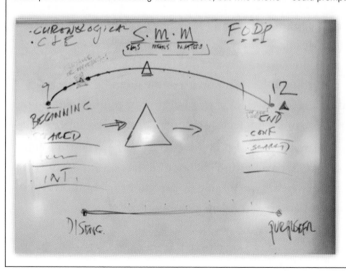

FIGURE 1–13 *Continued*

© 2019 by Jim Burke from *The Six Academic Writing Assignments*. Portsmouth, NH: Heinemann.

Over the course of the next month, when students wrote, they wrote only in the Digital Daybook. Here is a representative sample of some of the entries I assigned for their *1984* Digital Daybook:

- ► Generate questions and respond to ideas about power.
- ► Speculate about what the world will be like in fifty years.
- ► Respond to questions for Chapter 1 in *1984*.
- ► Write a fifteen-minute essay about Orwell's ideas about power throughout Book 1 of *1984*.
- ► Summarize Chapters 4–5 from Book 2 of *1984*.
- ► Interpret the poem "Walls," by South African poet Oswald Joseph Mtshali; then explain how it applies to Winston and Julia in *1984*.
- ► Watch and then summarize and respond to Karen Armstrong's argument in her TED Talk about compassion; then explain whether or not Winston's response to Julia's fall is or is not compassionate according to the ideas Armstrong spells out in her TED Talk.
- ► Research (quickly!) the story of the Garden of Eden and then find support in the specified pages for the claim that Orwell's language suggests Winston and Julia are akin to Adam and Eve and this scene is an allusion to the story of the Garden of Eden. Be sure to include specific passages from the text to support your thinking.
- ► Create a two-column table, putting "Literal Meaning" in the header of the left column and "Figurative Meaning" in the header of the right. Working with a partner (but each creating your own entry in your Digital Daybook), list three items from the story that you think are important to the meaning of the story (see my example of the glass paperweight); then in the right column, explain the figurative meaning of the item (again, see my example for the glass paperweight).
- ► Summarize French and Raven's types-of-power model from the Wikipedia entry in a well-organized paragraph, paying close attention to the transition words you use when comparing the different types of power. Explain which of these types of power best captures the nature of O'Brien's power in the chapter you read last night.
- ► After looking at the political cartoon about President Trump and *1984*, explain what point the cartoonist is trying to make and why.

- ▶ Watch and then analyze the Apple *1984* commercial, often considered the best commercial of all time, and explain what it is trying to say about the Apple computer and its debut in 1984 and how Jobs' vision of Apple differs from George Orwell's in *1984*.

- ▶ Write the sort of brief synopsis (about fifty words) you would find on Netflix for the movie *The Lives of Others* after watching it.

- ▶ On a sheet of paper, jot down connections between *1984* and the movie *The Lives of Others* as you watch it. Anything you write in one column should have a corresponding connection in the other.

- ▶ Photograph your list of connections between the book and the film; then send the image to yourself and paste it into your Digital Daybook. Then, choose one of the connections from your list and write about how Orwell and the filmmaker treat that idea in the movie and the book, making sure you provide examples from each to support what you are saying. (See the example in Figure 1–14.)

As you can see from these different tasks, the students wrote about a wide range of topics, all of which were designed to help them not only better understand the novel but also improve their abilities as academic readers, writers, and thinkers. Often, the entries here were done at the beginning of the period and would then serve as the basis for small-group or full-class discussions about their ideas and how they related to the book. As others have suggested, students tend to write more and find working on the computers more engaging than if they were doing the same work by hand. While this is likely true, a number of studies have begun to suggest that students who take notes on computers remember and understand much less than those who do so by hand, which requires students to process and prioritize content before jotting down the key information. Regardless of the specific approach, one must design the assignment in such a way that it conforms to the Academic Writing Assignment Framework mentioned in the previous section and elsewhere; otherwise, the task risks being busywork in the eyes of the students and, as a result, ineffective.

The tasks here are, generally speaking, intellectually demanding but informal in their spirit: most are done in the opening minutes of the class to establish the focus and momentum for the period. Assessing all this writing requires little time and effort because I am skimming through it all to check their thinking and effort. In the example that follows, the assignment is much more structured and represents a more deliberate means of teaching academic reading, writing, and thinking throughout much of the fall.

May 22: *The Lives of Others*

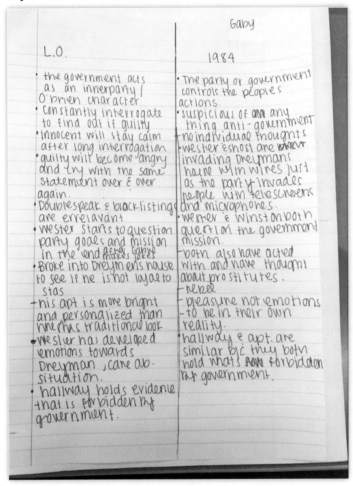

1. The movie takes place in Berlin. An officer named Gerd Wiesler doubts a famous playwright's loyalty to the Communist Party. He gets permission to spy on him and his actress-lover Christa-Maria. Wiesler becomes unexpectedly sympathetic to the two that he is spying on and starts to face conflicting loyalties when his superior takes a liking to Christa-Maria and orders Wiesler to get the playwright out of the way.

2. Common themes between *1984* & *The Lives of Others* : Privacy, Love, Questioning, Authority, Forbid, Emotion, Invasion.

3. The one theme that I think connects *1984* and *the Lives of Others* the most is emotion. In both *1984* and *The Lives of Others*, people lack emotion and consideration of other people's feelings. The Party controls the people so much that they are forbidden from feeling empathy, love, compassion, creativity and more. The book is made around how Winston and Julia break this set idea of having no emotion. In *1984* the point is to get rid of feeling and anything other than the thought of the party, by contrast, the movie doesn't have the same objective. Feeling and emotion is grown in Wiesler through experience and sympathy. Initially, Wiesler acts as someone without heart. Technically he is monitoring the couple for actions against the government, but in reality, he is really there to monitor against a feminine energy that entertains the heart, as well as the mind, when considering the meaning of experience. The couple's humanness, their creativity and passion, and their love for each other stimulated Wiesler's imagination and his feminine, more feeling side. By the end, Wiesler becomes a whole, integrated being of feeling and reason. He becomes a man who feels, simply because he was privy to the feeling lives of others. Similar to this, Winston and Julia start to develop the same feelings once they escalate their love for each other in *1984*. The parallel between these two stories is that feeling emotion and possessing things such as sympathy, compassion, love and creativity, isn't easy; it requires effort and a yearn to feel. In *1984* that year was breaking the rules, however in *The Lives of Others* it was through experiencing and developing an open mind to other people.

FIGURE 1–14 Though students generally do their writing *in* their daybook, we sometimes need to work by hand. In this case, students took two-column notes to compare a film and a novel and then snapped a photo of those notes and embedded the image into their written response to the film.

Critical Notes

The Expert Project paper is a major assignment that marks the culmination of a yearlong inquiry into a topic that students choose early in the fall semester of their senior year. An important part of that process includes giving students the time and opportunity to explore different topics in order to discover the topic they will investigate. However, there is a second, equally important part of that initial topic exploration process: diving in, going long and deep with the topic once they choose it. Through this process of unpacking their topic, students discover what they really find interesting about that subject and how much more complex their topic, regardless of what it is, is than they first thought. Central to this discovery process in the fall is an assignment, almost weekly for much of the fall semester, called Critical Notes.

A very structured assignment, Critical Notes asks students to respond to a series of ten questions designed to address different aspects of the text they read that week. Students can read pretty much any type of text each week: images, videos, songs, Twitter or other social media feeds related to their topic, online or print articles, podcasts, and TED Talks. The only real constraint is that they should not just watch a TED Talk each week; instead, they must examine their topic from different angles through different media by way of further understanding their topic and what they want to examine about it through longer, book-length texts they must then read on their own and about which they must write in-class timed essays each grading period.

The Critical Notes assignment itself is designed with several key elements in mind. First, it is designed to be distributed, displayed, and done online, so it comes to students as a Google Doc through Google Classroom. It is the same template each week; this is important, as it helps students, especially those who struggle, realize that what seems daunting at first quickly becomes familiar once they finish the first couple of assignments. What looks like a really long assignment is deceptively manageable: all the demands of the assignment and the guidelines appear in the left column; the space in which they must write their responses is on the right. One reason I design and distribute the Critical Notes as a Google Doc is that students will, when working on paper, fill in only the space you give them in a box. On the digital assignment, the boxes expand to accommodate students' writing, thus allowing and encouraging them to elaborate on their answers. Another is that it enables me to embed links to useful resources, models, and other documents when necessary.

Critical Notes

These answers all conform to the WTL guidelines discussed in this chapter insofar as the emphasis is on using writing to help them think about the text they read and learn more about the topic they are exploring. Embedded within the Critical Notes assignment, however, is a series of thinking and writing moves fundamental to the academic enterprise. Throughout the semester, I routinely provide support for those students who need more guidance, who need to know what it looks like to evaluate a text and its source, for example. Students also have access to completed Critical Notes about all different types of texts they might read, which include, in addition to those listed earlier, political cartoons, commercials, advertisements, video games, and more—anything that functions as a text rich with meaning about their topic. Numbers 1–9 on the assignment sheet are designed to prepare them to write number 10 (see Figures 1–15a and 1–15b), the one part of the assignment that makes more formal demands when it comes to writing but still serves as an appropriate part of this WTL assignment.

When I first introduce the Expert Project and the Critical Notes portion of it at the beginning of the year, I take several days to do so, walking them through each element, providing the rationale for it and giving them models, which I explain in detail. In the subsequent weeks, I take some part of the Critical Notes that the class, or some subset of it, is struggling with and discuss it in depth as a form of feedback on both their writing and their thinking. Number 10 inevitably proves to be most challenging, so one year, I selected a strong example from a student and heavily annotated it using the comments feature in Microsoft Word (which I prefer for this purpose over the same feature in Google Docs) and then uploaded it as a pdf, to which they had a link they could use the rest of the semester. As the example in Figure 1–16 shows, I used the formatting features of Microsoft Word (bold, italics, highlighting) to draw out and comment on different aspects of what Anna Utrata was doing so others could improve in those areas the following week. By providing such detailed feedback on one student's paper, I was doing the same for all, as this was an area of weakness for nearly everyone. When I presented the annotated model, students accessed the document, which I had made available as a link in the Daily Record for that day, on their Chromebooks while I displayed it on the overhead screen so I could point out specific details as I explained my comments on Anna's example.

When students come in on Monday mornings during the fall semester, they gather into groups roughly related to their topics—those investigating performance-enhancing drugs might be joined by those studying addiction, and so on—and use their Critical Notes as the basis for small-group discussions, after which I might ask them to write a bit more in their daybooks about what new questions or connections they have about their topics. In this way, the student that begins an inquiry about performance-enhancing drugs might realize, after hearing other students talk about Lance Armstrong or students abusing Adderall to help them in school, that what he or she is really investigating is not performance-enhancing drugs as much as it is cheating and why people do it.

Name: _____ **Period:** _____ **Date:** _____

Overview: Use this template to write up your Critical Notes each week. It is designed to be written on a computer, so the area where you type your response will expand to accommodate your writing.

BEFORE YOU BEGIN READING	
1. Clarify and State Your Purpose **a.** I am learning about _____ **b.** because I want to find out whether _____ **c.** in order to help my reader understand that _____.	**1. Clarify and State Your Purpose** (**Yes**: *Write it out each time whether it's the same or changes.*) Type your response here . . .
2. Write a Properly Formatted MLA Citation Author(s). Number, Title of the source. Publisher, Title of container,[1] Publication date, Other contributors, Location. Version,	**2. Write a Properly Formatted MLA Citation** (*Click here to learn the correct* MLA citation *for your source.*) Type your response here . . .
3. Evaluate the Text and Its Source: Is this text: ☐ current (up-to-date, still true) ☐ relevant (related to your topic) ☐ credible (accurate, trustworthy)	☐ substantive (important, interesting) ☐ legitimate (in terms of length, tone, quality) ☐ new information, type, source, or media format

4. Orient Yourself: Scan the Text and Create a PQ
☐ Scan the title, subtitles, features to get the gist.
☐ Develop a purpose question (PQ) *before* reading to
 	
    clarify what is important to notice
    focus your attention and be more purposeful
    assess your understanding when you finish
	4. Orient Yourself: Scan the Text and Create a PQ
	
	Type your response here . . .

WHILE YOU ARE READING	

5. Identify and Capture Key Ideas, Claims, Evidence
Jot down those details or passages most relevant to your PQ or EP topic. Focus on how or why the author
 	
    defines or establishes his or her message
    creates and conveys this message
    makes and develops his or her primary claim
    states these claims (the author's motive)
    uses logic and evidence support any claims
    chooses and uses examples/other supporting details
	5. Identify and Capture Key Ideas, Claims, Evidence
	
	Type your response here . . .

6. Acknowledge and Address Alternative Views
Identify and discuss who would disagree with ideas or positions in this text and how to address their concerns.
 	
    Who might disagree with this position?
    Why might these people or groups disagree?
    How would you summarize their position?
    How would you answer or address their position?
	6. Acknowledge and Address Alternative Views
	
	Type your response here . . .

[1]**Container** is a strange term in a citation. It refers to where the text you are citing appears such as the name of a professional journal, a collection of stories, a website of a professional organization, and so on.

FIGURE 1–15a The Critical Notes handout comes as a Google Doc students can write directly into as they explore their Expert Project topic and develop a critical sensibility for how to read about their subject. All their writing is done on the right side; on the left, you see the guidelines for what they must do.

(*continues*)

7. Analyze the Medium, Means, and Message This is a very important element of any text you read: People choose the medium and means that best allow them to deliver their message with the intended effect. Consider: Who created this message or text? Why did he or she create or send this message? Who is the intended audience? Who benefits most from this information? What technique does the author use to achieve his or her purpose? What groups, values, lifestyles, or points of view does this message represent, leave out, or dismiss?	**7. Analyze the Medium, Means, and Message** Type your response here . . .

AFTER YOU FINISH READING

8. Respond, Reflect, and Connect
 	
Respond to the author's claims by
    a. agreeing—but with a difference
    b. disagreeing with reasons
    c. agreeing *and* disagreeing
 	
Explain and support your response with your own reasoning, evidence, and examples.
Discuss how this author's ideas and claims connect or compare to previous readings.
	8. Respond, Reflect, and Connect
	
	Type your response here . . .

9. Evaluate Importance: So What? Who Cares? People always wonder, "What's your *point*?" or "What does this have to do with *me*?" **So what?:** Why does the author's point matter? **Who cares?:** To whom does this matter most?	**9. Evaluate Importance: So What? Who Cares?** Type your response here . . .

10. Write a Rhetorical Analysis of the Text You Read, Viewed, or Heard (#10 is the most valuable!)

Write your analysis here. (**NB**[2]: This box will expand to accommodate your writing; that is, your analysis should be fully developed, with a clear focus, effective organization, and insightful commentary.)

Type your response here . . .

Check Your Work

My work on this assignment is

- ☐ **Complete:** I have done all the steps above.
- ☐ **Correct:** I proofread and formatted my work; I used proper grammar, punctuation, and capitalization.
- ☐ **Coherent:** I showed that I understand the key ideas of the text and its connection to my topic.
- ☐ **Consistent:** My work here is as good as or better than the work I have done on similar assignments.

Grade/Feedback

---

[2]**NB:** Latin for: *nota bene*; it means that one should take special note. (It is used to precede a written note).

FIGURE 1–15b *Continued*

Critical Notes Explained: Numbers 1-9 prepare you to write a detailed rhetorical analysis in #10

Note Number 10 is the most demanding and important part of the Critical Notes since it requires you to synthesize all the elements and ideas you take notes about in numbers 1-9. In addition to the following new directions for #10, you can find additional help at the Bakersfield College website, which features tips, templates, and additional examples.

10. Write a Rhetorical Analysis of the Text You Read, Viewed, or Heard

If you write by hand, I suggest using a separate sheet of paper and attaching it so you have room to write. Your analysis should include or discuss: (1) the focus (subject + what author says about it) of the text; (2) the structure (how ideas and details are arranged to achieve the author's purpose), (3) the author's claim, reasoning, and evidence; (4) the methods the author uses to achieve that purpose; and (5) how effectively the author's message was conveyed. (6) Finally, you should include your response (do you agree, disagree, or both agree *and* disagree?) and reasoning behind it. The following example, written by Anna Utrata, offers us a more local example of what a well-written and insightful analysis looks like:

#10. *In an article titled* "New Study Links Weather Extremes to Global Warming," *New York Times* writer Justin Gillis **reports** on new studies linking weather patterns to global warming. *Before the industrial revolution,* Gillis **observes**, these weather patterns were not as extreme. *Yet after looking at the data,* Gillis **shows** there is a clear connection between climate change and green house gases and the pollution that increasingly threatens our atmosphere. *Specifically,* Gillis **describes** how researchers discovered the earth has warmed by 1.5 degrees since the 19th century. *Although this doesn't seem like a big number,* the report **warns** that the earth will continue to get hotter in the foreseeable future. Many people disagree with such claims that these changes in temperature are linked to global warming, something Gillis **addresses** by acknowledging that "such heat extremes as the recent Chicago heat wave are still rare, which makes them difficult to study in a statistical sense." *Even so,* Gillis **counters** such doubts by describing how the ice caps have melted, causing sea levels to rise, which the studies attribute to global warming. *Although the climate changes do not, as yet, directly affect the areas we live in,* his point is that the problems are still happening and, according to these latest reports, growing more urgent. *Through his use of statistics and anecdotes drawn from his extensive interviews of experts from a range of backgrounds,* Gillis **illustrates** for his readers what the future will look like if we do nothing. *Thus* his purpose is two-fold: to **explain** what is happening and **to persuade** us to think and act differently in the future to prevent it. *Given his status as an award-winning reporter for the New York Times,* Gillis **exhibits** an authority and objectivity that demands that we listen since he has no other motive than to report what he learns through his investigations in the field and conversations with scientists from different countries.

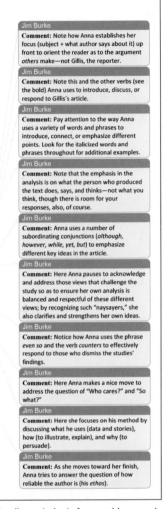

Jim Burke
Comment: Note how Anna establishes her focus (subject + what author says about it) up front to orient the reader as to the argument *others* make—not Gillis, the reporter.

Jim Burke
Comment: Note this and the other verbs (see the bold) Anna uses to introduce, discuss, or respond to Gillis's article.

Jim Burke
Comment: Pay attention to the way Anna uses a variety of words and phrases to introduce, connect, or emphasize different points. Look for the italicized words and phrases throughout for additional examples.

Jim Burke
Comment: Note that the emphasis in the analysis is on what the person who produced the text does, says, and thinks—not what you think, though there is room for your responses, also, of course.

Jim Burke
Comment: Anna uses a number of subordinating conjunctions (*although, however, while, yet, but*) to emphasize different key ideas in the article.

Jim Burke
Comment: Here Anna pauses to acknowledge and address those views that challenge the study so as to ensure her own analysis is balanced and respectful of these different views; by recognizing such "naysayers," she also clarifies and strengthens her own ideas.

Jim Burke
Comment: Notice how Anna uses the phrase *even so* and the verb *counters* to effectively respond to those who dismiss the studies' findings.

Jim Burke
Comment: Here Anna makes a nice move to address the question of "Who cares?" and "So what?"

Jim Burke
Comment: Here she focuses on his method by discussing what he uses (data and stories), how (to illustrate, explain), and why (to persuade).

Jim Burke
Comment: As she moves toward her finish, Anna tries to answer the question of how reliable the author is (his *ethos*).

FIGURE 1–16 This detailed annotated example took me some time but served as feedback to all my students for a problem most of them had; it also then served as a model for students in subsequent years and so, ultimately, saved me time.

When the semester ends and students must write an interim paper about what they have learned so far about this topic and what they think about it, it is the Critical Notes that prove most useful. And when they transition in the spring to create their big presentation on their topic prior to writing their final paper, they find it was the Critical Notes that helped them most, all of which end up included in their annotated bibliography when they finish their Expert Project.

Obstacles and Opportunities

Because of the more flexible, informal nature of WTL assignments, obstacles pose less trouble than on more structured, conventional assignments, which can carry a higher penalty as a consequence of such obstacles. As our focus throughout this book is design, it makes more sense here to speak of WTL obstacles as constraints one must consider when creating such assignments. When we design WTL tasks, which tend to serve as preparation for other, more major assignments, we face constraints of time but also more affective constraints related to engagement. That is, if students feel the WTL work is busywork, something that serves no real purpose, the writing assignment will not accomplish much. Or if students find no personal connection to their own experience or culture, or sense some bias in the task that runs counter to their values or views, they will likely give little to and get even less from the assignment.

Again, because WTL assignments are never the primary goal of our instruction, we face added constraints we might call both linguistic and cognitive, for if the assignments are too difficult or require too much in the way of directions, they will demand time we probably do not have. Obvious exceptions exist, of course, the Critical Notes being such a case; however, if you were to look at the tasks for all the entries in the Digital Daybook, you would find that most of them are easily explained either verbally or through written directions I provide online through the Daily Record.

As I have discussed the role of technology and my students' use of our class set of Chromebooks, it is worth mentioning that technology—the availability of the hardware and access to the software—poses another constraint for some teachers when it comes to creating WTL assignments. Most of these assignments, however, can be done as easily and just as well with sticky notes or index cards as they can with Pear Deck or Socrative, to name just two of the ever-growing number of apps and online services out there, almost none of which I use with my students. The truth is, sometimes we end up using more time than we should when technology gets involved, thus rubbing up against the enduring constraint of time.

If the obstacles are few, though real, the opportunities WTL provides teachers are many and substantive. Just about any major study of secondary-level writing instruction of the last decade or two has found that students are not writing enough. WTL assignments, as this chapter has shown, offer a wide array of different tasks that teachers can design to complement their curriculum or integrate into the writing process for other academic writing assignments they design. Such assignments create important opportunities to increase engagement and improve students' agility and fluency as writers by having them write for a purpose but doing so with the freedom to safely try new approaches, styles, and strategies.

As I have shown throughout this chapter, WTL assignments offer key instructional opportunities to target specific areas of need such as reading comprehension and classroom discussion, as well as critical thinking—all areas where students need to be challenged and given opportunities to improve if they are to become the nimble, fluent, and confident writers they need to be in life. WTL assignments have enabled me to make much better and more intentional use of the class computers I have, allowing me to have students not just write a variety of forms and formats, but to write about the wide array of text types the computers have permitted us to read, watch, listen to, and view.

The central point running throughout this book is that, through our academic writing assignments, we are designing experiences meant to inspire and improve, to engage and educate our students. WTL assignments focus on those daily, often small but important experiences we can and should provide our students within the context of our larger curriculum. In a blog post titled "How Do You Make a Good Reader?" Timothy Shanahan (2017) identifies three aspects of experience as fundamental to such improvement: amount, content, and quality. As we design our WTL assignments, these three aspects of experience offer us a useful, efficient guide that suggests we should focus on the *amount* of experience (how much, how often, how long students write); the *content* of experience (what students write and write about, as well as the forms, features, formats, and functions of that writing); and the *quality* of experience (how well the assignment is designed to deliver the content of the lessons as well as the meaning and importance to students of the experience the assignment provides).

More than writing to learn, I want my students to use writing to *think*. In her studies of secondary literacy practices, Judith Langer found that one of the characteristics of the most effective teachers was that they taught students how to be generative thinkers (2000). When people in the workplace express concern about employees' readiness, it is often their ability to *think* that quickly emerges as the greatest concern. WTL assignments cultivate the intellectual agility, creativity, and fluency that thinkers in all fields—from Darwin and Einstein to da Vinci and Thomas Edison, Marcus Aurelius and Winston Churchill to business and thought leaders Tim Ferris and Tumblr founder David Karp—need if they are to do great and interesting work. Through such writing, one "can enhance the brain's intake, processing, retaining, and retrieving of information . . . promote the brain's attentive focus . . . boost long-term memory, illuminate patterns, give the brain time for reflection" (Oppong 2017). What more could we hope for from a writing assignment designed to help students learn?

Reflect on Your Own Practice

Take some time to consider the different types of WTL assignments I have discussed in this chapter and how they compare with your own classroom and curriculum. Specifically, I suggest that you do the following steps in your head, in writing, or as part of a discussion with members of your department or those instructional teams (sometimes called PLCs) to which you belong.

1. Generate a list of all the different WTL assignments you have students do in a semester or during a specific unit you just finished or are about to begin. You might take a minute to examine the assumptions behind these different assignments or the degree to which they complement other, larger assignments in your overall curriculum. Make notes as needed about ways you could improve your use or the design of WTL assignments based on your observations.

2. Examine the assignments on the list you created or a smaller subset of representative assignments in light of the AWA Framework checklist provided earlier in this chapter to assess the degree to which these writing assignments include or could be improved to better incorporate the features listed on the AWA Framework.

3. Review your list of the different WTL topics and tasks you made, paying specific attention to the verbs you ask them to do when writing; think of these as the mental moves or cognitive demands you are asking of your students. For help with improving these tasks and the verbs, check out the Webb's Depth of Knowledge model I created.

Webb's Depth
of Knowledge
Model

2 The Short Answer

*Fostering the Art of Paying Attention
and Close Reading*

I didn't have time to write a short letter, so I wrote a long one instead.

—MARK TWAIN

The Short-Answer (SA) Assignment: What It Is and Why We Assign It

Our greatest constraint in teaching in general and writing in particular is time. My classes meet four days a week: three times for fifty-one minutes and once for ninety. But we bleed time daily through the small intrusions from outside, through the time spent trying to get all the laptops distributed—or online, once they are in the kids' hands. Some years back, I kept track of every minute taken from my instructional time for a year, everything from the student interrupting to deliver summons notes from the counseling department to mandatory state testing days, extended lunch times for prom fashion shows to assemblies and rallies. By year's end, I had lost a cumulative total of roughly twenty-eight hours, which added up to over thirty class periods if I used my fifty-one-minute period as a point of reference. As Don Graves used to tell me, "teachers are like five-pound bags into which people are always trying to stuff ten pounds of grain." That is, every year we are asked to fit more into our class time—school wellness surveys, counseling visits to schedule next year's classes, fund-raisers for a range of different initiatives—but never given more time to teach what students are expected to learn.

Perhaps it is this crush of time that accounts for the dominance of short-answer (SA) writing assignments in grades 6–12 and college. Applebee and Langer defined such assignments as less than a paragraph in their national study of writing in grades 6–12

(2013). Perhaps it is the lack of time that explains why, of the 8,542 assignments Apple-bee and Langer analyzed, only 19 percent were "extended responses" (a paragraph or longer), with the remaining 81 percent of the writing assignments described as fill-in or short-answer exercises—or what they refer to as "writing without composing" (13). Perhaps college professors feel some similar variation of this pressure, as well, for in his study of college writing assignments, Melzer found that short-answer writing assign-ments and assessments were the most common type of writing assignments among the 2,101 he examined (2014, 22).

Obviously, other explanations for the prevalence of the short-answer assignment exist, all of which we understand and accept as legitimate, given the constraints of time within which we work and the challenges we face. The paper load. The push to prepare for vari-ous state exams that require such short writing. The need to monitor and assess students' understanding and progress. The need for time to practice certain writing moves and ways of thinking through such short assignments.

What do these short-answer assignments look like? What do they demand? When, how, and why do we tend to design and assign these short-answer writing tasks? While Applebee and Langer, for the purposes of their cross-disciplinary study, defined an ex-tended piece of writing as a paragraph or longer, my working definition here will be that such short-answer assignments are a paragraph or less. Of the hundreds of mostly high school assignments I collected over a three-year period, the short-answer work served as a form of note-taking in many cases, assessment in others, writing practice or reading strat-egy in still others. With these examples in mind, another constraint of the short-answer task appears to be the cognitive demands of such representative assignments as these:

- ▶ In a clear sentence or two, explain how each of the themes listed below is demon-strated in the text. The best answers will include specific, relevant examples from the text as well as a clear explanation of how and why they demonstrate the theme at hand. [Note: The handout provides students with a box 0.75 inches high in which to do this.]

- ▶ Explain how this paragraph is an example of ethos. Restate what _____ says and why it is an appeal to ethos. [Note: The handout provides two lines in which to do this.]

- ▶ Describe the events and list the characters involved in Act 2.5. [Then, in a sepa-rate box with a space measuring two inches by one, it adds the following.] Make inferences, predictions, or draw conclusions [then lists sentence starters such as *I think . . .* , *I noticed . . .* , *I predict . . .* , *I question . . .*].

I indicated how much space was provided for the students' answers to the questions to illustrate how short-answer assignments often want to accomplish much more than they allow students the space to do so. Increasingly, we face questions about how best to format and deliver these questions—on paper or through an app of some sort? And, if digital, then should we use a generic Google Doc or a more specialized app such as InsertLearning, which allows teachers to format online content, including articles on a site like www .nytimes.com, with boxes for students to embed their comments about such articles and questions right in the article as they read it online?

For the purposes of academic writing assignments, including short-answer tasks, Wilhoit observes that "at the heart of every [academic writing] assignment is the rhetorical situation—someone writing to someone about something for some purpose" (2002, 62).

What Students Say and How They Struggle with SA Assignments

If, as Wilhoit insists, all academic writing assignments are anchored in some rhetorical situation, these tasks give students plenty to struggle with in the process of writing them and teachers no less to grapple with when designing and grading them. Given that the typical short-answer writing assignment results in no more than a paragraph of writing, teachers often risk "presenting [students] with an overwhelming task" (Melzer 2014, 50) that demands serious thinking and cannot be answered in a few sentences. As Melzer writes, this most common writing assignment is "the genre most lacking in rhetorical context"; moreover, these assignments "leave no room for personal connections [and] benefit students least in terms of making meaning and [helping them to enter] into the conversation of their discipline" (52).

With Melzer's critique in mind, consider the following example from an assignment for *Lord of the Flies*. Students receive a handout with twelve questions to answer about Chapter 1; however, upon closer inspection, one realizes there are *twenty-five* questions for Chapter 1 alone, since each item has two or three questions hidden within it like Russian nesting dolls. Here is one example from the list of twelve questions about Chapter 1:

5. What do Piggy and Ralph find in the water? How do they feel about it?
   Whose idea is it to use it to call the others?

This pattern of roughly twelve questions per chapter (that are really twenty-five questions) is sustained across all the subsequent chapters on similar handouts. By the end of the book, then, students will have written approximately 300 short-answer responses to questions like these, many of which students could write at least a paragraph about and few, if any, of which have any meaningful connection to each other or to the students responding to them. It is also reasonable to assume that most of these answers could be found online; what's more, few students would be likely to feel guilty about asking friends to share a few answers. Another assignment for *Lord of the Flies* narrows the scope and the number of questions, asking students to respond to the same five questions for each chapter:

1. What is the meaning of the chapter's title?
2. Describe the most significant events of the chapter. Bullet points are fine, but be specific and complete.
3. Who are the most important characters in this chapter?
4. What's the most significant moment in this chapter? Why?
5. What is the most crucial symbol in this chapter? Why?

What will students struggle with when writing about such prompts? First, they find it hard to engage with the questions, to attach any meaning to them beyond their value as assignments that will be graded. In other words, they often see such questions, which can often be answered by consulting online resources such as Shmoop, as busywork. Reflecting on his son's experiences with reading in the current age of distraction, where time and attention seem to grow more fragmented all the time, David Ulin wrote about his fifteen-year-old son, Noah, and his experience of reading *Great Gatsby*:

> Part of the class structure involved annotation, which Noah detested; it kept pulling him out of the story to stop every few lines and make a note, mark a citation, to demonstrate that he'd been paying attention to what he read. "It would be much easier if they'd let me *read* it," he lamented. (2010, 1)

My point is not that we should not have students respond to or write about or take notes on or annotate what they read (though twenty-five questions for one eighteen-page chapter of *Lord of the Flies* is a bit much); rather, my concern here is that we remember we are designing *an experience*, one that shapes not just what and how our students will learn but also how they will feel about literature, reading, writing, and our course. Ulin's son Noah put it this way: "This is why reading is over. None of my friends like it. Nobody wants to do it anymore" (8), a feeling Kelly Gallagher has termed "readicide" (2010). Gallagher writes:

On my desk is a copy of the Los Angeles Unified School District's guide to teaching *To Kill a Mockingbird*. This guide contains overarching questions, chapter study questions, essay questions, vocabulary lessons, activities for specific chapters, guided reading lessons, directions for setting up a writer's notebook, literary analysis questions, collaborative activities, handouts, transparencies, twenty detailed lessons, quizzes, and projects. The guide is 122 pages long and includes numerous pages listing goals and "habits of thinking" that teachers should foster in students.

Why is this guide so exhaustive? Because it's aligned to the massive number of standards found on California's standardized exams each spring. As a result, teachers are driven into a "teach all things in all books" approach.

I am not suggesting that the goals in this unit of study are not worthy; they are. But using *all* these lessons to teach one novel, which teachers must do if they are to prepare their students for standardized exams, is a recipe for readicide. If I were to follow this curriculum guide step-by-step in my own classroom, there is little doubt my students would exit my class hating *To Kill a Mockingbird*—and possibly all reading—forever. (38)

But those students who do the short-answer work thoroughly, responding to all the questions in depth, have a different problem: how much to write when they could write so much about just one of the twenty-five questions for Chapter 1 of *Lord of the Flies*? Worse yet, in my experience, is the student, often one with learning difficulties, who spends one or two hours doing something we assumed would take fifteen or twenty minutes when we wrote up the questions. One way I check my assumptions on such assignments is, periodically, to ask students to write down how long they spent on the assignment when I collect it. When a hardworking special-needs student like Lourdes writes "two hours" up in the corner, I cannot help but wince and apologize to her the following day, insisting she not spend more than some agreed-upon and reasonable amount of time on those assignments that will follow. Better that we should keep in mind the experience we are designing for all our students and be guided by the sort of thinking that informs Kelly Gallagher's approach:

When I teach *1984*, it doesn't overly concern me that some of my students are not going to like the novel. What concerns me is that all my students understand the value of the reading experience. As they read George Orwell's classic, I want my students to gain awareness of government surveillance today. I want them to understand that the torture site "Room 101" is not simply limited to Orwell's world—that many believe it has been re-created in Abu Ghraib and the detention center at Guantanamo Bay, Cuba. I want them to recognize the degree of language manipulation and propaganda they will confront for the rest of their lives. But I must make this value visible *before* my students commence reading. In introducing novels like these, I always address the central question my students bring to the book: Why should I care? (2010, 39)

As Gallagher and Noah, the student mentioned earlier, make clear, the greater challenge is designing short-answer tasks that meet the guidelines outlined in this abbreviated version of the Academic Writing Assignment Framework, by being

- ▶ anchored in clear goals linked to specific standards;
- ▶ grounded in texts that are engaging and demanding;
- ▶ cognitively demanding;
- ▶ emotionally and intellectually engaging to all students;
- ▶ designed to support students;
- ▶ assessed or evaluated according to criteria and requirements that are clearly stated; and
- ▶ written and formatted for maximum readability and ease of use.

The last item, regarding the usability and readability of the writing assignments and their directions, can be especially important on these short-answer tasks, given their frequency of use and the number of demands that can be baked into just one task or a night's homework that includes many more, as the *Lord of the Flies* example shows. This means careful attention must be paid not only to how the assignment is formatted (i.e., if you want students to respond in depth, they need room to do so) but to what is required and the directions that spell out those requirements. A quick glance down pages and pages of such short-answer assignments reveals a clear and narrow set of writing and thinking moves common to most of these assignments: *identify, describe, summarize*; moreover, those tasks framed as questions often begin with *what* or *who* instead of words such as *why* or *how*, which are more likely to make greater cognitive demands consistent with level 3 or level 4 on Webb's Depth of Knowledge model.

Webb's Depth of Knowledge Model

When questions are more specific, complex, and text-dependent when referring to the text, students are likely to struggle, because such tasks integrate the reading and writing processes. That is, students who struggle to read closely will inevitably fumble in their response when writing since they cannot write about what they do not understand well. On the other end of the continuum, short-answer assignments can be more open-ended, calling for more generative and critical thinking, as with these questions students asked prior to reading and discussing *The Great Gatsby*:

What is the purpose of marriage?

How does desperation affect one's morals or standards?

Why do people associate money with happiness?

To what extent do people define themselves by their economic status?

What can't money buy?

True, these questions are part of an anticipatory set of questions designed to help the teachers frame *Gatsby* and prime students' cognitive pump. Still, the aim here is to design short-answer writing tasks that engage and prepare students to read and grapple with some of those "central questions" that Gallagher mentions and Fitzgerald asks. No doubt the teachers will follow up such a thoughtful introduction with questions designed to further support such an inquiry and nurture students' interest in the text.

The Forms and Features of SA Assignments

As with most of the other types of writing assignments, the forms of short-answer writing assignments can sometimes overlap, most often with writing-on-demand (WOD) and writing-to-learn (WTL) assignments, discussed in other chapters. Yet there are clear distinctions that mark the short-answer assignment as a specific type, one that we design and treat differently than we do those WOD and WTL assignments we create. While WOD assignments typically assess students' understanding and abilities, often in an essay form, short-answer assignments are neither timed nor given the same weight; thus short-answer tasks rarely inspire the sense of dread or anxiety WOD assignments do. As for WTL assignments, they may ask students to do certain similar tasks, but these actions are more likely to be done in a notebook or another informal context; short-answer assignments, however, more often get collected and graded in some form as students do them. In other words, there is a greater degree of accountability for each specific short-answer assignment than students would expect with WTL work that was either not collected or would be graded only later as part of the work of one's notebook in a class.

As I have already mentioned, some of the greatest concerns with the short-answer tasks students are assigned have to do with the demands they make on students and how engaging students find the work of such assignments to be. Applebee and Langer summed up their critique of short assignments by saying that the tasks amounted to "writing without composing" (2013, 14). With this criteria in mind, we might think of short-answer tasks arrayed along an informal continuum, with *composing* at one end and *copying* at the other and such words as *capturing* and *creating* falling somewhere in between. Keeping these criteria in mind, I offer a few representative short-answer assignments that seem to challenge and engage while preparing students for the demands of college, where, according to Melzer's study (2014), our high school graduates will find many similar assignments:

Rhetorical
Précis Notes

▶ *The Rhetorical Précis:* A rhetorical précis asks students to take notes on what an author does and says about a subject and then use these notes to write a paragraph in which they discuss their insights about what the author says, how and why the author says it, and how it relates to the subject of the text. As students read the specified text, they jot down notes that correspond with the précis template, which they then use to write a rhetorical précis, as Wyatt, a student in my AP literature class, did about William Deresiewicz's essay titled "Solitude and Leadership":

> In his essay "Solitude and Leadership," delivered as a speech to the graduates of West Point, William Deresiewicz claims that in the face of bureaucracies and peer pressure, the dynamic between solitude and leadership serves as the ideal platform for finding ourselves and helping the world to make progress. He extends this claim by first emphasizing the style of today's bureaucratic leaders and how they promote the status quo, rather than change it. Then, Deresiewicz personalizes the issue by adding the importance of intimacy through solitude and, ultimately, how time to think in such a space will lead to becoming a different type of leader. His purpose is to appeal to the West Point audience in order to secure the future and change the norms of leaders that he vehemently opposes. Deresiewicz establishes an urgent tone by highlighting their military concerns and addressing and refuting opposing views. His conclusions are significant to today for his words provide us, and his audience, with a new lens through which we can see and discover new aspects of ourselves so that we are moved to answer the call-to-action behind his words.

▶ *Rhetorical Notes:* In order to help students read closely but not disrupt their experience of reading a longer work, such as *The Immortal Life of Henrietta Lacks*, I have them capture key details using the Rhetorical Notes tool I designed. It asks students to write one sentence at the end of each chapter. Here are the directions:

> After reading each chapter in *Henrietta Lacks*, pause to think about the author's purpose regarding the different subjects we have generated. Then, complete the next line on the Rhetorical Notes sheet below that corresponds with the chapter you just read. *Each line should read as one complete sentence all the way across*, as the example below shows. Include punctuation as needed to make the sentence correct. After each section (e.g., the first eleven chapters) in the book, you will write a one-page analysis as directed, using the notes and ideas from the previous chapters to guide you.

An example of the Rhetorical Notes handout, which they receive and complete in Google Docs, is shown in Figure 2–1.

Directions: After reading each chapter in *Henrietta Lacks*, pause to think about the author's purpose regarding the different subjects listed on the Story Lines handout. Then complete the next line on the Rhetorical Notes sheet below that corresponds with the chapter you just read. Each line should read as one sentence all the way across, as the example below shows. Include punctuation as needed to make the sentence correct. Then, after each section (e.g., the first eleven chapters) in the book, write a one-page analysis as directed, using the notes and ideas from the previous chapters to guide you.

CH	WHO	DOES WHAT	TO WHOM OR WHAT	HOW	WHY
	Subject	*Verb*	*Phrase or Clause*	*Phrase or Clause*	*Phrase or Clause*
PART ONE: LIFE					
Prologue	Rebecca Skloot	begins	her book *The Immortal Life of Henrietta Lacks*	by focusing on who Henrietta Lacks was and what she contributed to modern genetics,	so that she can argue that without Lacks' cells, solving most major health problems would not be possible.
1					
2					
3					
4					
5					
6					
7					
8					
9					
10					
11					

Directions: Using the sentences, notes, and observations above from Part One, write a one-page analysis of Part One (Prologue–Chapter 11) in which you make a claim about the topic and what Skloot has been saying about and trying to accomplish regarding that topic in Part One. Include evidence from the book and your notes.

(continues)

FIGURE 2–1 Rhetorical Notes sample for *The Immortal Life of Henrietta Lacks*

© 2019 by Jim Burke from *The Six Academic Writing Assignments*. Portsmouth, NH: Heinemann.

CH	WHO	DOES WHAT	TO WHOM OR WHAT	HOW	WHY
	Subject	*Verb*	*Phrase or Clause*	*Phrase or Clause*	*Phrase or Clause*
PART TWO: DEATH					
12					
13					
14					
15					
16					
17					
18					
19					
20					
21					
22					

Directions: Using the sentences, notes, and observations above from Part Two, write a one-page analysis of Part Two (Chapters 12–22) in which you make a claim about the topic and what Skloot has been saying about and trying to accomplish regarding that topic in Part Two. Include evidence from the book and your notes.

FIGURE 2–1 *Continued*

CH	WHO	DOES WHAT	TO WHOM OR WHAT	HOW	WHY
	Subject	Verb	Phrase or Clause	Phrase or Clause	Phrase or Clause
			PART THREE: IMMORTALITY		
23					
24					
25					
26					
27					
28					
29					
30					
31					
32					
33					
34					
35					
36					
37					
38					
Afterword					

Directions: Using the sentences, notes, and observations above from Part Three, write a one-page analysis of Part Three (Chapter 23–Afterword) in which you make a claim about the topic and what Skloot has been saying about and trying to accomplish regarding that topic in Part Three. Include evidence from the book and your notes.

FIGURE 2–1 *Continued*

Listener's
Notes

► *Listener's Notes:* In order to improve students' ability to listen to and understand what they hear in a lecture or talk (e.g., TED Talk) and then convey that understanding and their response to the speaker's arguments in a way that holds them accountable while developing their writing skills, I have students fill out Listener's Notes, which I distribute as a Google Doc, while they watch a video, such as Carol Dweck's TED Talk titled "The Power of Believing You Can Improve."

► *Author's Notes: Says–Means–Matters (SMM):* A tool I designed to direct students' attention when reading for both meaning and importance, Author's Notes is a structured note-taking tool created to improve students' ability to read for the "So what?" of a text in any medium, something students find difficult to do. Also, it gives students a measure of choice about what parts of and ideas in a text they choose to examine, which increases the likelihood of greater engagement. (See Figure 1–11.)

► *Questions for Close and Critical Reading:* Questions are one of the primary drivers of short-answer assignments, especially when we want to target instruction to specific writing and thinking moves in response to complex texts. A range of approaches exist, but the ones that can be used in a variety of contexts and show consistently strong results are Question the Author (Beck and McKeown 2006), Question Formation Technique (Rothstein and Santana 2011), Question-Answer Relationships (Rafael, Highfield, and Au 2006), and Text-Dependent Questions (Fisher and Frey 2014). You can find abundant examples and resources online and through their books to help you adopt or adapt their ideas for your students in general or a particular text you are preparing to teach.

The examples I just discussed share one feature, as do many of the assignments you will find throughout the book: you can adapt or adopt them for use on just about any text you teach, for any class, at any level. By designing such tools and techniques, I can focus on how to teach the skills needed to read, write, and think at the levels appropriate to the assignment and students' grade level. They also allow for a quiet, informal differentiation by challenging all to enter and work up from wherever they are as readers and writers toward where I expect them to be eventually. As designed, these different approaches work well as preparation for subsequent papers, presentations, or other types of culminating writing assignments for the current unit. One last benefit deserves consideration: Such generic strategies, of which there are many more than the few I discussed, save me important time that I can spend preparing for upcoming lessons, designing other units, grading papers—or, dare I say it, getting in some time on the bike, with my family, or with a good book I want to read for the sheer pleasure of reading a book I will not have to teach.

In the section that follows, I explore in greater detail examples of questions and how I use some of these tools and techniques in my own classes. The best of these questions and approaches include choice whenever possible. They also make a point, as we see with the four stages in Fisher and Frey's model, of ensuring that the questions students write about are progressively more demanding and anchored in the texts they are trying to analyze and understand.

The examples discussed here follow the guidelines, perhaps more difficult for short-answer writing assignments because of their brevity, outlined here in this abbreviated version of the Academic Writing Assignment Framework, which asks us to design questions that are

- ▶ anchored in clear goals linked to specific standards;
- ▶ grounded in texts;
- ▶ cognitively demanding;
- ▶ emotionally and intellectually engaging to all students;
- ▶ designed to support students;
- ▶ assessed or evaluated according to criteria and requirements that are clearly stated; and
- ▶ written and formatted for maximum readability and ease of use.

Classroom Connection: What SA Assignments Look Like in My Class

My education in designing questions and prompts for readers and writers is not a pretty one. It comes with many mistakes, most of which are punctuated with apologetic responses to frustrated students that are all different versions of, "Oh, sorry! I didn't realize or think about that!" When working through the process of developing questions for all the readings in *Uncharted Territory* (2017a), an anthology I edited for W. W. Norton, I finished all the questions and felt very satisfied with myself. That was, until we had someone who really knows a lot about the language, logic, and sequencing of questions examine a few sample sets and he said it looked like someone had yelled, "Go find me a bunch of questions!" In other words, he was saying the questions had no clear aim and even less logic in terms of what they asked and how they were arranged. So, just when I thought the book was finished, I felt compelled to redo them all. And he was, of course, correct. The revised set of questions was made better by the creation of a structure that allows teachers and students to choose whether to assign or respond to all or some of the short-answer questions. Here is a sample set of questions that accompany Robert Frost's "The Road Not Taken":

Navigating the Waters: Reading Comprehension

1. What is the first decision the speaker must make in the poem?

2. Why does the speaker decide to take "the other" path? Support your answer with evidence from the text.

3. What do you think the speaker means in line 14 when he says, "Yet knowing how way leads on to way"?

4. How does the speaker think he will feel about his decision "ages and ages hence"?

Exploring the Depths: Rhetorical Strategies and Structures

1. Frost frames the poem as being about a decision, which the speaker then explores. What is the decision and how does Frost organize the poem in response to or as a result of this decision?

2. How does Frost describe the "two roads [that] diverged in a yellow wood"—and to what end? Cite specific passages from the text to support your ideas.

3. Identify all the points where the speaker in the poem must make a decision then discuss the language Frost uses to frame that decision. The first example would be in line 2 where the speaker says, "sorry I could not travel both / And be one traveler."

Sharing the Discoveries: Discussion and Writing

1. This poem is often read at commencement ceremonies. Explain why this poem might be a good or a poor choice for graduation. Refer to specific passages from the text to support your response.

2. Frost, in describing the roads, stresses that "the other [road was] just as fair and having perhaps the better claim," and so decides to take the one that "was grassy and wanted wear" though it was, when compared with the other road, "really about the same." Reflect on the different paths you could choose among at this stage of your life. Are they all similar or would one of them be more likely to make "all the difference" when you look back on it years from now?

3. Did the road the narrator chose actually make a difference, or is the narrator telling himself this for another reason?

Though this is the three-tiered structure we developed for the Norton anthology, the larger point is to ensure the questions assigned have some sort of logic and structure to them. In general, I use the following structure when developing questions for my classes:

KEYWORDS

These words appear in the assigned text or will prepare students to read it.

LEVELS

1. *Before Beginning to Read:* These are questions used to prime the pump (activate connections in the reader's brain) before reading, to frame the text within a larger inquiry or purpose. These questions may apply to the reader's own experience, previous texts studied, or concepts the reader needs some background knowledge of to read the text successfully. These questions might also relate to the genre or medium if either is new to the reader and thus requires some contextualization or explanation.

2. *On the Surface:* These are literal or factual questions one can find answers to on the page. They are comprehension questions that show that students understand the basic gist of the text. These questions emphasize skills such as identification and description; in other words, reading on the surface level means reading for what you can see, what people do or say.

3. *Below the Surface:* These questions mirror those on the SAT, ACT, AP, or state standards exams, as they emphasize close reading. This means students analyze and evaluate language, organizational structures, author's purpose, rhetorical strategies, genre conventions, and matters of craft. In other words, the answers to all below-the-surface questions are found *within* the text and thus require readers to make inferences and draw conclusions they can support with evidence from within the text itself.

4. *Above and Beyond the Surface:* These questions involve critical reading and thus ask students to make connections with other texts, current and historical events, their own experiences, or different critical theories such as postcolonial or feminist theory that often take the reader outside the text in order to help him or her think about the text from different perspectives or through a different lens.

LENSES

Another approach is to invite students to examine the text from different perspectives or through different critical lenses: economic, historical, psychological, philosophical, sociological, gender, cultural, racial, or postcolonial.

My education in crafting great short-answer questions for students to write about is far from over. As I insist throughout this book, however, the design thinking approach invites us to treat our work as an ongoing prototype we are always testing and refining through the feedback of students' performance and what this tells us about our own. One question the short-answer assignment demands we ask is: Why should we have students write at all if we can achieve the same end, gain the same insight into students' performance, through multiple-choice questions that can be scored and returned in the click of a key? Or, put another way: What does writing do that such machine-scored multiple-choice questions cannot?

I have felt a steadily increasing pressure from different sides, as I suspect we all have, to incorporate more technology, to use less paper, and to provide more accountability, more formative feedback to students about their performance. I have challenged myself in both short-answer writing tasks and multiple-choice questions to see if it is possible to accomplish more than the basic check for understanding (without overwhelming myself in the process with the grading of either type of question). It is *1984* that has provided me the greatest opportunity in the last few years to experiment with short-answer questions that challenge and engage without intruding, I hope, on students' reading experience.

Figure 2–2 shows the directions and sample questions I provided students, via Google Classroom as a Google Doc, for Chapters 1.4–1.5 of *1984*.

These questions provide choice and, in my experience for the last few years, short-answer writing tasks that are both engaging and challenging. In addition, they consistently support rich discussions at both the whole-class and small-group level. The paragraph at the end, not meant to take them more than fifteen minutes to write, lays the foundation for one of the essays they can choose to write at the end about the different types of power French and Raven spell out in their model. My goal was to create questions that would make demands on them as writers but also require them to think about what they read; also, I wanted the questions, as I just mentioned, to support a productive and engaging class conversation that also, if we were lucky, would prepare the students to write an essay at the end of the unit that could use ideas from or perhaps even include the paragraphs themselves.

Obstacles and Opportunities

The obstacles and opportunities we face most constantly are those inherent in the short-answer assignments themselves. We run this gauntlet of demands, each year given what often seems like a whole new load of them to carry with no more time in

Directions: *Answer any three* of the questions listed below *and write the required draft paragraph* at the end.

Chapters 1.4–1.5

1. Reread the discussion about "truth" and "facts" on pages 40–41. Generate three questions one can ask to determine (in our world today) with certainty if something is true (i.e., a fact). Explain briefly how each question allows one to determine if something is true—and why you would be vaporized for even thinking, let alone asking, those questions.

2. Which of the following diagrams best represents the relationship between people in Oceania? Explain why that diagram best illustrates the nature of the relationship.

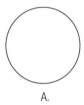   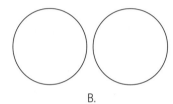   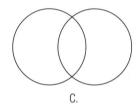

A.   B.   C.

3. Read the following claim and respond as directed below:

> "The woman with sandy hair" (42) is complicit in the systematic murder of thousands because she "tracks down and deletes from the press the names of those who have been vaporized."

Explain why you (a) agree with the claim, (b) disagree, or (c) agree *and* disagree. Provide examples from the text to support your response.

4. **Part A:** Define the word *orthodox* as it appears in the dictionary.

   Part B: Apply the idea of orthodoxy to two people at Winston's workplace, explaining how it applies (i.e., where would they fall on a continuum of orthodoxy?).

5. On page 61, Winston lists all the people who he thinks will be "vaporized." What criteria for being vaporized (or avoiding that fate) can you infer from his list?

Required Response: Draft Paragraph

1. Identify and discuss which one of French and Raven's six types of power is most central to this chapter.

2. Make a claim about what Orwell is saying—directly or indirectly—about this type of power.

3. Support your claim with reasons and evidence from the text. Explain how your quotations support your claim.

FIGURE 2–2 Sample questions from *1984*

which to do so. Technology, so ripe with opportunities for us, simultaneously creates new hurdles of time with all that we must learn and do to prepare for and use it in ways that make a difference.

As I have tried to show in this chapter, it is possible to design short-answer assignments that challenge and engage students if they are created with those ends in mind. However, other studies serve to remind us what we are up against in this area. The 2011 NAEP found that 10 percent of eighth graders and 14 percent of twelfth-graders said they had done "no writing for their English language arts classes for homework in a typical week"; moreover, the same report found that 31 percent of eighth graders and 26 percent of twelfth-graders reported writing a page or less in a typical week of work in class (Applebee and Langer 2013, 13).

Short-answer assignments can accomplish much; yet they are not complete writing performances. Rather, they are little more than opportunities to learn, rehearse, or practice the moves students must learn as academic readers, writers, and thinkers. They are also opportunities, if we make them so, to light a fire in the minds of our students as they enter into the conversations of the texts we teach. If we do not treat them as such opportunities, these short writing assignments will be little more than empty vessels that students are asked to fill—and fill they will, most likely with the words of those they find online and with the resentment we heard in the voice of young Noah earlier in this chapter when he said to his father, "Reading is over. None of my friends like it. Nobody wants to do it anymore" (Ulin 2010, 8).

Do I think reading is over? Of course not. I share with Penny Kittle the hope that by helping students engage meaningfully with texts and questions they care about, we can empower them, as Penny says as part of her credo on her website:

> I believe each of my students must craft an individual reading life of challenge, whim, curiosity, and hunger. I believe in the collecting, noticing, living work of designing lessons to empower writers. (2018)

Reflect on Your Own Practice

Take some time to consider the different types of short-answer writing assignments I have discussed in this chapter and how they compare with your own classroom and curriculum. Consider doing the following steps in your head, in writing, or as part of a discussion with members of your department or those instructional teams (sometimes called PLCs) to which you belong.

1. Generate a list of all the different short-answer writing assignments you have students do in a semester or during a specific unit you just finished or are about to begin. You might take a minute to examine the assumptions behind these different assignments or the degree to which they complement other, larger assignments in your overall curriculum. Make notes as needed about ways you could improve your use or the design of short-answer assignments based on your observations. If you have explored the boundary between multiple-choice questions and short-answer questions, as I did in this chapter, what were your motives, observations, and conclusions?

2. Examine the assignments on the list you created or a smaller subset of representative assignments in light of the AWA Framework checklist provided earlier in this chapter to assess the degree to which these writing assignments include or could be improved to better incorporate the features listed on the AWA Framework.

3 Writing on Demand
Finding an Authentic Pathway for Learning

> *When it came down to writing the timed writing assessment, hands were being raised left and right with questions. It was the simple questions that concerned me the most: How do I start? What should I write? What is this asking me to do? What should my conclusion paragraph say? What should I write next? "I can't think" was the mantra chanted through each class period.*

> —SEVENTH-GRADE ENGLISH LANGUAGE ARTS TEACHER

Writing on Demand (WOD): What It Is and Why We Assign It

Writing on demand (WOD) is as artificial as it is essential to our students' academic success. As one of the most common and, therefore, consequential types of academic writing, WOD is a key to the kingdom we all want our students to enter. If they cannot achieve some degree of confidence and competence when it comes to WOD assignments, those students we worry about most will be denied the opportunities that come to those who can do well on the SAT or ACT, take an in-class final without fear of failing, and ace the state or AP exams when they get to the writing section. Our challenge is to create timed writing assignments that engage our students in meaningful ways while at the same time teaching them the essential skills common to the assignments and assessments that fall under the heading of writing on demand. In other words, we must keep in mind that we are designing not just an academic writing assignment but an experience, an assessment, and a document that should clarify, not confuse or unnecessarily consume the time of our students.

Writing on demand goes by many names, of course, all familiar but not interchangeable: timed writing, constructed response, in-class essay, essay exam, writing assessment. Whatever the name, we all know the feeling of pressure and, for some, anxiety that comes with writing under the gun of the clock. For the current generation of students, timed writing assessments are all too familiar as a result of increased emphasis on state testing and standards. Yet such timed assignments also appear like clockwork in Advanced Placement classes, making the DBQ (document-based question), FRQ (free-response question), synthesis questions, and style analysis questions staples of all AP courses.

In addition to these AP practice exams, which often constitute a large part of a student's grade and appear on final exams, record numbers of high school students now take the SAT or ACT exam, both of which include demanding academic writing tasks students must complete within the allotted time. Many teachers are actually required to integrate SAT or ACT exams into their standard curriculum now that these assessments serve as state exams in a growing number of places. Finally, some teachers require students to write all papers and other important writing assignments in class while the faces of both the clock and the teacher watch over the students; these teachers see this approach as a way to guard against plagiarism and long papers that would take more time to grade. Some districts go so far as to forbid any writing assignments that do not directly mimic and thus prepare students for state exams, most of which feature WOD tasks.

As you might imagine, such an overemphasis on timed writing and test preparation does little to prepare students for the demands of college writing and even less to engage students or provide a context for robust and meaningful writing instruction. Still, these assignments are part of the world in which we work and for which we must prepare our students. The question is: Can we create timed assignments that prepare our students and, at the same time, engage the head (logic), heart (emotions), and hands (skills, or what the Greeks called *techne*, which refers to craft)? As this chapter shows, I know we can, but only if we create such assignments by design.

What Students Say and How They Struggle with WOD Assignments

Though there are ways to incorporate revision or a more process-based instructional approach, as we will see in the chapter on writing process papers, writing on demand tends to emphasize content over craft, substance over style, performance over process. It is, in short, a type of writing students must do if they are to go to college. One of my senior students said when reflecting on timed writing: "I've become adapted to timed writing from all the FRQ, DBQ, AP testings, SATs, ACT. However, I am not a big fan of them. I don't think timed writing is an accurate representation of who I am as a writer."

For a small group of students, writing on demand is like a shot: It only hurts a bit and is soon over. Most students, however, would rather *receive* a shot than suffer the anxiety of timed writing. The rest of us fall between these two poles, our degree of anxiety largely depending on how prepared we feel for the stand-and-deliver moment of the timed writing assignment, which usually serves as an assessment, an opportunity to show what you know in a specified period of time. One of my students, when asked about timed writing, observed, "Timed writing assessments are stressful. Students, including myself, often feel pressured to write more quickly and focus less on the quality of their work. I am a slow and methodical worker. I like to take my time to ensure the quality of my work. It is so hard to prepare for these assessments. Timed writing requires a different set of skills than traditional writing."

Other students I surveyed appreciated all the things that troubled this student. For example, one said: "I actually don't think timed writing is that bad. I can't spend too much time on it and there is only so much I can do to prepare for it. So there's no reason for me to think that I have spent too little time writing it. Also, revision is not my strongest suit and in timed writing I'm not expected to revise. This helps me stress out a lot less about timed writing because there is only so much I can do. ☺"

In my survey of over one hundred of my college prep senior English students, nearly all of them ranked "timed/in-class writing on a topic or text that requires analysis" as the most difficult type of writing assignment. When we factor in such growing and troubling trends as the rise in anxiety and depression, learning difficulties, other special needs, and the challenges of English learners and chronically disengaged students, we quickly realize what a minefield timed writing assignments can be.

The Forms and Features of WOD Assignments

But what forms do such timed writing take in most classes and what are the features such assignments most often include? Aside from essays of one sort or another, WOD tasks focus on constructed responses, paragraphs, and such localized forms as the "extended paragraph," which is usually just a page-long response. Some, including state essay exams, require students to write more real-world forms such as letters (to a local official, school board member, or administrator) and editorials such as one might write for the newspaper. An increasing number of institutional writing performances, in accordance with the growing emphasis on argument writing and close reading of nonfiction texts, require our students to write what are variously referred to as synthesis essays or simulated research papers. Similar to the DBQ for the AP social studies exams or the synthesis essay for the AP English language assessment, these assignments demand that students not only write on demand but do so about a selection of texts of different types, which they must first *read* on demand (i.e., under the pressure of time and for a predetermined purpose) for the arguments and general quality of the reasoning and evidence in the texts.

As you might expect, given these different timed writing tasks, we first have to decide whether we will create our own writing assignment; use those provided by the publisher of the textbook we use or an online service such as ThinkCERCA or NextLesson; or choose a released exam from the College Board, ACT, state department of education, or some other institution to which we are all accountable. Instead of adopting such writing assignments outright, some of us adapt these WOD assignments to meet our own or our students' needs in order to address the relevant skills or standards; not all of us, of course, are free to make such tweaks to our assignments. Still, studies suggest that when we can exercise some choice, no matter how small, in the curriculum of our courses, we and our students feel a greater sense of engagement, voice, and ownership (Langer 2014, xxi).

Both the SAT and the ACT are battling it out to gain a foothold in our classrooms, where they and other state standards agencies insist they are trying to assess more of what actually happens in the classroom. One way to do this is by providing, as the SAT does, a template for the type of timed writing students will actually do on the SAT, which combines academic reading, analysis, and writing. Such academic writing, according to the College Board, emphasizes three different domains: reading, analytical thinking, and, of course, writing. More specifically, such writing serves to assess how well students comprehend and can use evidence from the source texts to convey their understanding of the author's "central ideas, important details, and their relationship," while also showing that they can organize their ideas into a logical progression that is clear, concise, and consistent in tone and command of the conventions of standard written English (College Board 2014, 75).

Here is the template the College Board provides for the redesigned SAT writing prompt:

Directions

As you read the passage below, consider how [the author] uses:

- evidence, such as facts or examples, to support claims
- reasoning to develop ideas and to connect claims and evidence
- stylistic or persuasive elements, such as word choice or appeals to emotion, to add power to the ideas expressed

Write an essay in which you explain how [the author] builds an argument to persuade [his/her] audience that [author's claim]. In your essay, analyze how [the author] uses one or more of the features listed above (or features of your own choice) to strengthen the logic and persuasiveness of [his/her] argument. Be sure that your analysis focuses on the most relevant features of the passage. Your essay should not explain whether you agree with [the author's] claims, but rather explain how the author builds an argument to persuade [his/her] audience.

What would it look like to use such a template to develop a timed writing assignment for my students? If I were to incorporate this template into the curriculum for my seniors during our *Into the Wild* unit, I would do so when students read "Where I Lived" from Thoreau's *Walden* as part of our inquiry into the idea of a credo by which one should live his or her life. Using the redesigned SAT prompt, I could create either a practice or an actual writing assignment after they read Thoreau that looked something like this:

As you read the passage below, consider how [the author] uses:

- evidence, such as facts or examples, to support claims
- reasoning to develop ideas and to connect claims and evidence
- stylistic or persuasive elements, such as word choice or appeals to emotion, to add power to the ideas expressed

Directions

Write an essay about Thoreau's "Where I Lived" in which you explain how Thoreau builds an argument to persuade his audience that they should "simplify, simplify, simplify!" In your essay, analyze how Thoreau uses one or more of the features listed above (or features of your own choice) to strengthen the logic and persuasiveness of his argument. Be sure that your analysis focuses on the most relevant features of the passage. Your essay should not explain whether you agree with Thoreau's claims, but rather explain how he builds an argument to persuade his audience.

As I said before, we are not always free to choose our own or tweak others' writing prompts, of course, as the following sample WOD assignment reminds us. As you read it, pay attention to the language, the demands, and the assumptions made about what students know and are able to do as well as the issues related to engagement and motivation it raises for these seventh graders—and their teacher.

Directions

The following prompt relates to the accompanying two sources by Sandra Cisneros and Walter Dean Myers.

This question requires you to synthesize (combine) a variety of sources into a coherent (clear), well-written essay that demonstrates your viewpoint (argument) on the issue. When you synthesize sources, you refer to them to develop your position and cite them accurately. The sources should support your analysis; avoid merely summarizing your sources. Cite sources consistently.

Writing Situation

An author creates a personality and assigns behaviors to create fictional characters. Authors also use setting and a character interacting with and within the setting to communicate thematic messages. The setting is the location and time frame in which the action of a narrative takes place. The two provided sources both demonstrate a similar theme of struggling against difficult circumstances and overcoming obstacles.

Writing Assignment

Using the two provided sources, compare and contrast how each author uses the description of the setting as seen through the eyes of the character to communicate a common thematic statement. Consider the similarities and differences of the physical setting, as well as how each character relates to his or her surroundings to overcome obstacles.

You may refer to the sources by their titles (Source A, Source B, etc.) or by the descriptions in the parentheses.

It is easy to imagine students' response to this. The academic language (*synthesis, viewpoint, common thematic statement*) makes it nearly impenetrable; for English learners, the directions will devour precious time that could be better spent writing. Ironically, all efforts to improve clarity—the addition of parenthetical synonyms such as *argument, clear,* and *coherent*—only undermine it; such efforts are particularly troubling given that a number of the helpful additions are simply wrong: *synthesize* does not mean combine; *coherent* does not mean clear; *viewpoint* does not mean argument. The important lesson here is that we are never just designing a prompt or a writing assignment; rather, we are designing an experience, a document, an assessment, a tool that students must be able to *use* without struggling to make sense of it or taking too long to read it.

In addition to being poorly written, such writing assignments are wooden stakes driven into the heart of an entire generation of students; however, to realize this is for seventh graders is to marvel that any of them would arrive in high school or college with a love of writing and the confidence that they could do it well and in their own voice.

Assignments such as this sample remind us that we are always teaching and designing writing assignments within constraints that are imposed on us either from above (the state, district, department) or through the context in which we teach (number of students, amount of time, available resources). Teachers who used this prompt, which had been developed by the county office and mandated by the district's principals, then scored students' papers using a 6+1 Traits rubric (one page with 872 words in an eight-point font, with five columns, seven rows, and eighteen bulleted descriptors spread across the seven traits, which are used to determine both the student's grade and level of performance). As schools throughout the district had, over time, each revised this "districtwide" rubric according to their own needs and using their own terminology, it is difficult to see how the writing assignment or the subsequent process would lead to any coherent or consistent approach to or discussion of writing in this district.

The Academic Writing Assignment Framework, discussed in previous chapters, offers the sort of guidance we need when designing, assigning, and assessing the different academic writing assignments featured in this book. The AWA Framework, the full version of which I include below to refresh your memory, reminds us that if our writing assignments are to be consistently effective and engaging, they must be

- ► *anchored in clear goals linked to specific standards* appropriate to students' age and development, as well as the future exams they will take in class, for the state, or on national assessments;
- ► *grounded in texts* that are as engaging as they are demanding in terms of how those texts must be read and used in the writing task;
- ► *cognitively demanding* relative to the standards themselves and students' intellectual progress without being overwhelming and thus leaving students feeling defeated;
- ► *emotionally and intellectually engaging to all students* to the degree that the assignments give students some measure of choice when it comes to the texts, tasks, and topics they encounter in the context of the writing assignment;
- ► *designed to support students* in ways that help them meet the challenges of the writing task while also demonstrating their knowledge and skills legitimately and independently despite such potential obstacles as language or learning difficulties;

- *assessed or evaluated according to criteria and requirements that are clearly stated* up front so students can use them as a guide and know how best to spend their time and energy when writing the assignment; and

- *written and formatted for maximum readability and ease of use* in language that is clear, consistent, concise, and correct, using a layout that makes clear what students need to do and how they need to do it.

Classroom Connection: What WOD Looks Like in My Class

If you were to visit my classroom, you would find a much greater emphasis on the other five types of writing assignments. This is not to say that students do not write on demand in my class. Specifically, I give my students the following types of timed writing assignments over the course of a semester, most of them written either at the end of the grading period or the semester:

- *Summer Reading:* We ask students to read a biography, autobiography, or memoir related to a person or a group of people worth studying. We also ask them to read an extended profile by Michael Lewis titled "Coach Fitz's Management Theory" from the *New York Times*. We designed the summer reading assessment to evaluate where students are as readers, writers, and thinkers without ending the first week with a stack of papers we have to read while we are busy getting the new semester started. Students can bring notes and their books; they write it by hand during the forty-five minutes allowed them.

Summer Reading Assessment

- *Independent Reading:* Seniors read two independent reading (IR) books each semester—two in the fall, two in the spring—all of them nonfiction and related to their Expert Project, a yearlong inquiry into a topic that culminates in a major paper (see Chapter 5 for more on this assignment). Students can bring their book(s), notes, and previous IR essays; use the Continuum of Signal Verbs handout and *They Say/I Say: The Moves That Matter in Academic Writing* (Graff and Birkenstein 2014); and refer to the annotated model of a similar IR essay made available online through Google Classroom. They usually write these IR essays in class on the computers and then submit them to Turnitin. Students have approximately an hour, depending on whether we are on a block or regular schedule on the day they write.

Continuum of Signal Verbs

Annotated Sample IR Essay

▶ *Major Works:* When reading major works such as *Wild, Into the Wild, The Immortal Life of Henrietta Lacks*, or *1984*, students typically take notes or write "chunks" of an essay about the book as they read it (a process explained in Chapter 4 and discussed briefly in Chapter 1). Only when we have run out of time to assemble and write a process paper do they write in-class essays about such major works. Students are permitted to bring their book, notes, and all chunks they have written along the way; they may use the book *They Say/I Say* (Graff and Birkenstein 2014) and any other handouts I have provided to help them write such a paper. They write it on the computer and submit it to Turnitin. Students get about an hour, depending on the schedule at school that day.

▶ *Simulated Research:* Borrowing from the example of the AP English language synthesis paper, this in-class paper marks the culmination of a unit that requires students to read a range of different texts, mostly nonfiction, some graphic or quantitative, occasionally a primary source or two. They come to class having done all the readings and have the two-hour period of the final exam to write it or the ninety-minute block period to write their simulated research paper at the end of the grading period. Students are allowed to bring and use all the readings for the unit and any notes they have made; they are encouraged to use *They Say/I Say* during the period. They are required to write the papers on the laptops and submit them to Turnitin, which doubles as a way to check for plagiarism and keep a digital portfolio of their work throughout the year.

Let's take a detailed look at one type of WOD assignment that figures prominently in my class throughout the year: the in-class essays students write about their independent reading books. In this particular instance, these are nonfiction books students chose themselves after getting them approved as part of their Expert Project proposal (which you can see and learn more about in Chapter 6). While I want to determine that students did, in fact, read the books and understand what the authors said about their chosen topic, I design the assignment with several other equally important aims in mind.

My own design process for such assignments begins with me asking questions commonly used throughout the design thinking process. Thinking of my students as users of the assignments I design, I start by asking myself what I know about them—their needs, interests, abilities—and how I can use that information to create an assignment that they will want to do and I will want to read yet will still measure their progress and assess their performance. In the sample assignment that follows, students choose to read two nonfiction books per semester as part of their yearlong exploration of a topic for their Expert Project. In addition to the choice of text (which they must get approved), they determine what they will write about so long as it focuses on what their chosen book says about their Expert Project topic (see Figures 3–2 and 3–3). Both teachers and students often struggle with this degree of freedom, yet it is consistent with the expectations of most colleges and the experiences of my own three children, who have passed through a range of two- and four-year colleges in recent years. My daughter, when she was a freshman in college, had a professor that would just say every three weeks or so, "Now write a five- to seven-page essay about some idea from the readings these last few weeks!"

Several other important questions arise at this point in the assignment design process, most of which relate to what designers call friction points in the user's journey throughout the assignment. In general, these can be understood as features of any interface that interfere with the user's ability to use the app, device, service, or process you've designed. The tendency in designers is to see all such friction points as bad, but for my purposes, whether a friction point is good or bad is more nuanced. Some friction points, for example, undermine students' performance by distracting them. These are the sorts of friction points we saw throughout the district-level prompt earlier. Other friction points are meant to nudge the students by prompting or reminding them to do certain things. This raises the question I must ask at this point every time I am creating a WOD assignment: How much support should I provide? You'll see several types of support in the assignment in Figure 3–1 that are worth discussing. First, I decided to put in the prewriting section to prevent them from just charging into the paper mindlessly. This is the sort of friction point that helps students orient themselves to the task ahead, reminding them that they have a destination. But I must constantly ask myself whether my efforts to clarify will only confuse my students more.

In addition to the support outlined in the previous paragraph, I make additional design choices at this point, some related to support. Because I have many kids with special needs of one sort or another, I tend to err in the direction of allowing multiple supports to all. This includes providing students with handouts such as the Continuum of Academic Signal Verbs; making available an annotated sample of a successful essay written in response to this same prompt (which they can access via the class laptops); permitting students to bring and refer to notes, annotations, and books, whether paper or digital; and encouraging them to use *They Say/I Say*.

Before I move past these initial questions about how much and what type of support to bake into the assignment, I need to pause and consider the more relevant constraints that apply to and might undermine some students' performance on the assignment. The most obvious constraint is, of course, time. This determines how much I can ask them to write and how much time they can spend reading the actual assignment sheet or using the various supports. Some constraints, such as how fast or how much kids can write in

Name: _____ Period: _____ Date: _____

Prewriting After putting your name, period, and date at the top of the page, do the following:

☐ **Express your Expert Project (EP) topic** in a word, a phrase, *and* a guiding question (GQ):
  ☐ **Word**: technology
  ☐ **Topic Phrase**: the effect of technology on our decision-making process
  ☐ **GQ**: How is technology affecting the way we think?
☐ **Write the title, author, year of publication, and number of pages** of your book.
☐ **Draw a line across the page** after you finish these prewriting items.

Directions Then, write an essay in which you do the following:
Please note: The following sections *do not* each equal a paragraph.

☐ **Introduce your subject,** discussing why you are interested in it, what other people say about it (e.g., in your Critical Notes readings), and what you have learned so far.
  ▶ See pages 303–5 in *They Say/I Say* if you need help introducing your subject.

☐ **Summarize the author's main idea or argument** regarding your EP topic/guiding question.
  ▶ See pages 305–9 in *They Say/I Say* if you need help summarizing the argument.

☐ **Identify and respond to the author's key ideas** by doing one or more of the following:
  ☐ agreeing—with a difference
  ☐ disagreeing—with reasons
  ☐ agreeing *and* disagreeing
  ▶ See pages 306–9 in *They Say/I Say* for help with identifying and responding to key ideas.

☐ **Acknowledge and address alternative/opposing views** about the author's positions/ideas.
  ▶ See pages 310–12 in *They Say/I Say* if you need help with acknowledging/addressing other views.

☐ **Draw conclusions about the meaning and importance of the book's claim(s)** as they relate to your topic and guiding question. In other words:
  ☐ Say what the author *says*.
  ☐ Explain what the author *means*.
  ☐ Argue why the author's position *matters* (or doesn't).
  ▶ See pages 312–13 in *They Say/I Say* for help with discussing the importance or meaning of ideas.

Assessment Your essay will be evaluated based on your performance in the following areas:

M = missed the standard   S = satisfied the standard   E = exceeded the standard

M	S	E	
☐	☐	☐	Introduce your subject and your motivation for writing about it.
☐	☐	☐	Summarize the author's main idea or argument (in IR 2) regarding your EP topic/GQ.
☐	☐	☐	Identify and respond to the author's key ideas by doing one or more of the following:
☐	☐	☐	Make a connection to your previous IR books (and, if possible, your primary research findings).
☐	☐	☐	Acknowledge and address alternative/opposing views.
☐	☐	☐	Draw conclusions about the meaning and importance of the book's claim(s).
☐	☐	☐	Prove that you read, understood, and thought about the book.
☐	☐	☐	Proofread and revise as time allows for correctness.
☐	☐	☐	Satisfy the requirements listed above to the best of your ability.

FIGURE 3–1 Handout for first Expert Project independent reading essay assignment

FIGURE 3–2 This student has his IR book out (an e-book he read on his phone), the annotated sample essay on the laptop screen as a guide, *They Say/I Say* for reference, and additional tools such as the Signal Verb Continuum at the ready.

FIGURE 3–3 As the IR books all relate to the Expert Project, this student has all the available resources plus some of her Critical Notes from the past weeks to help her connect her IR book to her Expert Project.

a given amount of time, are native to the territory of the type of writing, though those with 504 or IEP plans can request extended time and any other accommodations to which they are entitled. But I also need to stop to ask whether I am giving the English learners in the class the support they need. In part out of consideration for these students, I take time to verbally go over the directions and then follow up individually to make sure they understand what to do.

Returning to the assignment itself, the actual handout, I face still more decisions as part of the design process, all of which are unique to each assignment. Do I distribute the assignment sheet on paper or digitally, sharing it through a learning management system such as Canvas or Blackboard Learn or a program like Google Docs or Google Classroom? For me, paper is always the right choice in this situation, because I want students to be able to mark it up, make notes as they prepare to write, and check off what they have done as they write. But for timed writing, the computers pose other difficulties that are often best avoided: plagiarism, the siren call of sites that summarize books they might pretend they've read, and the fact that most state and other such tests are still written by hand. Some schools subscribe to services like Turnitin, which gives students the option to submit their typed papers to a digital reader for scoring and feedback, but this is not the reality or norm of all schools.

In this instance, because we had been working with many ideas from the high school edition of *They Say/I Say: The Moves That Matter in Academic Writing* (Graff and Birkenstein 2014), I anchored the directions and the assignment itself in the academic writing moves the authors suggest students use when writing about texts, specifically authors' arguments and how they do or do not apply to the claim students are making in their own paper. For the purposes of efficiency, I identified the associated moves for each section by listing the page numbers in *They Say/I Say*. Additionally, I provided bullets with the suggested moves they needed to make when they wrote the paper. Not everyone needed those; however, we cannot hope to see students make these moves if they do not learn which ones to make and how, when, and why to use them. Remember, the annotated example that students could refer to online corresponded to each of these sections; so students needing additional clarity and support could, for example, read over the example online to see what it looked like to "identify and respond to the author's key ideas."

The final design considerations for this and other such timed writing assignments? The document itself and the choices I have to make about layout, language, and assessment. Sections are always delineated by hanging indents that allow students to scan down the left margin and find what they need. I pay special attention to the verbs and any directions that tell students what they must do, for this is where we often cause the most confusion by using words the way the seventh-grade prompt mentioned earlier did. In addition, it is crucial to use such terms in ways that are consistent with the rest of the English department so as to avoid a Tower of Babel effect with academic language. To help students navigate the document, I leave plenty of space between lines (using 1.5 to 2.0 line spacing) and always choose fonts (Avenir, Calibri, Garamond, Cambria) and associated features (eleven- or twelve-point type, bold, all caps, italics, bullets, and boxes) that improve overall readability of the document. I make a conscious effort to use check boxes to indicate only those items or actions that are required; this way, the students know they need to be able to check off each of those items (see the Document Design Checklist).

Document Design Checklist

The assessment section, placed at the bottom, is designed to align with what I have emphasized at that point in the semester and what they need to learn; moreover, it is designed for ease of use since I am typically grading all these papers under the crush of the end of the grading period and have little time for specific feedback. Instead, I put sticky notes on a couple representative exemplary papers to remind me to copy them later; in addition, I jot down notes about common patterns—those to avoid and those to keep using—I see as I read through them all. When I return the papers, I will use the exemplary papers and these observations as the basis for my feedback to the whole class, encouraging those who wish to address more personal questions or concerns to meet with me outside of class so we can work through the paper together. It is, in short, a document designed to be helpful and easy to use—for both students and teacher! Were I teaching a class such as AP English or a lower grade that had much more responsibility to prepare students for the state exam, I would surely use a rubric or other means of scoring their papers that was aligned with the relevant standards and skills and include it on the back, while also making annotated sample essays available to them prior to or during the in-class writing assignment.

Sample AP Literature Rubric

After I return their graded papers, my students then have the assignment they will use—with the exception of the one added requirement—on the subsequent independent reading essays the rest of the year. Why do I do this? For the simple reason that I am not as interested in saying, "Gotcha!" as I am in saying, "You got it!" when it comes to making and mastering the moves of academic reading and writing. Keep in mind that I barely graduated from high school and spent time in a remedial writing course when I started at the local community college. For my own three children, the language and moves of academic writing were part of the air they breathed while growing up in a house where both parents were teachers. In my own house, however, I grew up loved and supported by a father who left high school after tenth grade and a mother who earned her high school diploma; so academic writing is not, in my experience, native to the majority of our students, especially those we worry about the most.

Subsequent IR assignments for the next three IR books vary only slightly from the guidelines and criteria for the first IR essay. The only change is that students must, in their subsequent IR essays, discuss the previous IR book(s) they read and how the ideas and arguments in those compare with the ideas and arguments in the book they just finished. The fourth and final IR essay, which comes near the end of the school year, asks students to write a letter to me in which they reflect on what the book they read told them about how they should live their life and how they have changed and grown as a reader over the course of the year, citing examples from the assigned IR readings to support their claims.

Obstacles and Opportunities

We all work in states, districts, schools, and departments with their own unique cultures, which inevitably include diverging positions and practices when it comes to the subject of writing on demand. Some teachers are constrained by district or department curriculum until the state tests are over in the spring; then, they are free to create their own writing assignments. Other teachers can create their own so long as they do so in collaboration with their professional learning communities (PLCs), which more or less describes how my fellow senior teachers and I work. Whatever your own situation, I have tried to offer a way to think about and approach timed writing that can help us all do a better job of addressing the aforementioned three Hs: the head (logic), heart (emotions), and hands (skills). Assignments that lack any one of these three ingredients stand little chance of making the difference we hope they will.

A timed writing assignment does not have to be terminal, an end point. As I discuss in greater detail in the next chapter, timed writing assignments can be turned into process papers if we design them with that end in mind. To do this increases the chances for improved writing instruction and deeper engagement, since students know it is not a "one and done" sort of assignment, but is, instead, one they have reason to invest in during the first stage as a timed assignment and later as a paper they will revise and have the chance to improve. Such an extended effort to revise and use that assignment as a means of teaching writing cultivates the sort of culture that elevates writing from a mere assessment to a major assignment, one that values craft as much as content. On a number of occasions over the years, I have had students write paragraphs about a theme as we read a book or collection of readings; then, on the day of the timed writing, I've told them to sift through these paragraphs to find three or four that worked as a unit, arrange them in a logical way, and write an intro and a conclusion. They've spent the remaining time in class refining and revising as time allowed, so the timed writing experience was more like a room full of quilters snipping and stitching away than a cage full of stress monkeys trying to scratch out essays with pens that were as useful as bananas.

If you detect an elasticity in my approach to writing assignments—extending timed writing assignments to include process writing, bailing on the process paper due to disruptions that leave us only time for a timed writing essay—you are right. Though we have always experienced some fluctuation from year to year, preventing one year's assignments from being a perfect fit for the following year's classes, my classes in recent years have presented new and unexpected challenges that demanded an unprecedented adaptability and agility on my part. While certainly a blessing, the class set of Chromebooks I now have in my class every day introduced an array of challenges that affected the time line of most assignments. In addition, the last few years have witnessed a rapid increase in the number of students identified as special needs or English learners; as a result, assignments often take longer than they once did as I work through the different recommended or mandated accommodations, especially those that apply to timed writing assignments. Moreover, the general push toward higher standards, whether from the Common Core or other state standards, has meant that many of us find assignments we may once have done in three weeks now take four or five weeks and so, as a result, the intended process paper is sometimes hastily reframed as a timed writing assignment because we have simply run out of time.

In the coming years, we will inevitably face the opportunity or, in some schools, the mandate to adopt writing systems that offer themselves up as complete solutions, something that will appeal to those under pressure at the higher levels of administration. Type in or click on a subject and the Swiss Army knife of some purchased program or platform will spit out the whole package—prompt, lesson plans, samples, and rubric—along with the option to have students upload the whole thing and get it scored and returned by the end of the period in which they create it. But such a solution will exacerbate the very problems it purports to solve, for it will, by removing the teacher from the process of designing and guiding students through the assignment, strip from our classes the culture and conversations that have the potential to make even timed writing assignments meaningful and, at their best, transformative.

I opened this chapter with the words of a young teacher who expressed her concerns about teaching the sort of top-down, overstuffed writing assignments those poor seventh graders had to complete. Let me end with a few more words from that teacher, for her sentiments highlight the obstacles and opportunities we all face when it comes to timed writing assignments:

> I'm concerned that my students haven't learned to actually think on their own. They've been conditioned through years in the education system to believe that confusion and asking questions results in answers being handed to you. They've learned that helplessness equals attention, and attention equals answers. And I want to break away from that.

She is not describing my classroom; nor, I hope, do you feel she is describing yours. Yet these are the pressures we all face, now and into the future. I hope the ideas in this chapter will help you, as they have for me, "break away" from empty assignments and use the framework outlined here to design not just assignments but experiences that will help your students write better and take pride in their work.

Reflect on Your Own Practice

Take some time to consider the different types of WOD assignments I have discussed in this chapter and how they compare with your own classroom and curriculum. Specifically, I suggest that you do the following steps in your head, in writing, or as part of a discussion with members of your department or those instructional teams (sometimes called PLCs) to which you belong.

1. Generate a list of all the different WOD assignments you have students do in a semester, whether you create them yourself or must ask your students to write them by mandate from your administration. You might take a minute to examine the assumptions behind these different WOD assignments or the degree to which they complement other, larger assignments in your overall curriculum. Consider drawing a pie chart to represent what percentage of your writing assignments fall into the WOD category. Make notes as needed about ways you could improve your use or the design of WOD assignments based on your observations and conversations with colleagues.

2. Examine the assignments on the list you created or a smaller subset of representative assignments in light of the AWA Framework checklist provided earlier in this chapter to assess the degree to which these writing assignments include or could be improved to better incorporate the features listed on the AWA Framework.

4 The Process Paper
Designing the Stages of Composing

When I'm asked to revise, I feel as if I'm being asked to revise myself.

—STUDENT quoted by Nancy Sommers in her blog *Between the Drafts*

The Process Paper: What It Is and Why We Assign It

Though most of the terms I am using to describe the different types of writing assignments are familiar, *process paper* is not a common term we all use. When I first began discussing the different types of writing assignments, people would say something like, "So a process paper is the same thing as an analytical essay," to which I would respond, "No, not really." The distinction I am making throughout this book is that these are the types of assignments we create—the ways we ask our students to work and write. Thus, a process paper *could* be an analytical essay, but it could be pretty much any other type of paper, even a personal narrative essay, that we had students take through the entire writing process. Applebee and Langer found that while most teachers believe they regularly take students through this process, they rarely do so as a consequence of "competing priorities, such as test preparation, [which] constrained the amount of time given to writing instruction" (2013, 21).

When we assign a process paper, we design an experience that takes students through a series of stages as they compose their papers. We are also creating an assignment that will take time—students' as well as our own—and demand a level of commitment and attention that we all struggle to muster and maintain. However, it is precisely such obstacles as engagement and stamina—our capacity to sustain our interest in an idea and the process of developing it over a period of days, weeks, or even months—that make the process paper such an important assignment to include throughout the school year. The process paper also offers students important opportunities to improve their writing in general and their performance on a given paper in particular. Yet there are those students whose experience has led them to loathe the writing process we promise will help them. When we tell our students they will be going through the whole writing process on this next paper, the jaded students think: "If you teachers *have* to assign a paper, why not get it out of the way with a quick in-class timed writing assignment?" They think of a writing assignment as a bandage one needs to remove: Just rip it off, instead of slowly peeling it away and causing all that pain and discomfort.

A process paper, however, provides us with the context and time we need to *teach* and improve writing; without the process paper in our curriculum, we are only *assigning* writing or *using* it to assess students' understanding of texts they read. If the process paper, with its different stages, gives students the chance to improve their paper, it offers us many chances to teach students the skills and strategies that, over time, develop in our students the independence, confidence, and agility they will need to meet the demands of longer and more complex academic writing assignments. When we design a process paper assignment, we are charting a course with many stops, each one specifically chosen to increase students' engagement and develop those skills, such as generating ideas and revising, with which students most consistently struggle. We are, in other words, a bit like travel agents who are asked to come up with an itinerary that both inspires and informs, teaches and transforms, but also manages to include stops and features that promise some fun. Along the way, we provide feedback like a helpful tour guide or an instructive Virgil to our young Dantes as they descend through the many circles of the writing process.

While this chapter focuses on designing writing assignments that follow a writing-process model, the truth is that most of the other six types of writing assignments can be adapted to some variation of the traditional writing process, even timed writing assignments. Research papers and most other long-form writing demand the discipline such a series of steps imposes, but as with all things that require discipline, we have to expect some students to resist or even reject the process. Alternative writing assignments, which incorporate most of the same basic academic forms and make similar rhetorical moves, certainly benefit from some version of the writing process, especially proposals, cover letters, or similar real-world forms that might well go out into the world to a live audience. The process for these different assignments follows a fairly well trodden path: Decide on a topic; find the information you need for the topic and task you've been assigned; come up with some plan for how to organize and use the information; then draft, revise, edit, and proofread your paper before turning it in.

Though these stages throughout the process are familiar, our focus here is on how to *design* such process assignments to include opportunities for feedback and revision along the way. As you will see, there are many possible iterations of the process paper, all of which I have assigned at one time or another. For example, in laying out the journey of the assignment, we can have students read assigned (or self-selected) texts straight through and then begin the writing process for the paper they will write. We can also direct students to read a text for some purpose or through some lens we assign or allow them to choose (e.g., critical theory, hero's journey, imagery, or a theme); this makes their reading more focused and purposeful as it anticipates the writing process that will follow. A third method I often use and explore later in the chapter integrates reading, writing, thinking, and speaking into a recursive process whereby students write a draft *as they read*, arriving at the end of the assigned reading(s) with a collection of paragraphs they can treat as a rough draft in need of an introduction, a conclusion, and a lot of revision.

There are many parts to any writing process; however, one of the defining characteristics is the challenge of coming up with and then refining and revising ideas and words, a process that takes time and patience but is essential to any writer's growth. Students are, in my experience, willing to work through such a process so long as they feel it will improve their writing and their paper (and, of course, their grade). Whereas we might assume they would grow bored soon after starting the process, I find the opposite: The more students work on the paper through such a process, the more they care, the more they feel a sense of ownership and pride in something they are taking the time to do well, as Ted, a senior in my class, wrote when reflecting on the writing process we used for a major research paper:

> As this paper was multiple steps, I felt that it allowed me to improve and take my time to carefully develop my ideas and correct my mistakes. I have learned ways to revise my paper from the strategies you taught us and different sentence structures from the book *They Say/I Say*, which really helped me get ideas about how to write. I never knew there were so many ways to write and all the feedback throughout the process helped me improve and feel more committed. After writing this paper, I think it also helped me get sorted out for my career path due to all the research and really finding my main interest. So not only has this process we followed helped me become a more skillful writer, but it helped me with my career path and things I can incorporate into my daily life as well.

In his comments about the process, Ted makes a case for why we need to return to the writing process throughout the year: It holds the power not only to teach but transform our students in ways that the timed writing assignment cannot achieve.

What Students Say and How They Struggle with Process Papers

When I surveyed my students about the parts of the writing process with which they consistently struggled the most, many responses were predictable but interesting nevertheless. Approximately 50 percent said they found it very difficult to generate ideas, revise, and proofread. Seventy-seven percent of respondents said their greatest struggle during the writing process was figuring out how to "manage [their] time, attention, and workload throughout the process (to avoid writing it at the last minute)." Roughly 80 percent said they were "more willing to revise if writing on a computer." In order to tease out their reasoning about revising, I gave them four quotes from Nancy Sommers (2012) and then asked them to choose the quotation that best represented their own attitude toward revision:

1. Revising is hard because you don't know if the changes you make are going to be better than the original choices.
2. When I'm asked to revise, I feel as if I'm being asked to revise myself.
3. When you revise, you are forced to think in ways you did not before.
4. Sometimes the first draft blocks a way of seeing something new.

The two top choices—the first and third—reflect students' divided mind, with about 45 percent choosing one, another 45 percent chose the other, and a much smaller but noteworthy number choosing the other two. Their choices suggest that the adolescent mind (and the developing writer's mind, as well) lacks the confidence and skill it will acquire over time when it comes to knowing what to change when revising, how to change it, and why it is the right change to make. We see this emerging faith in the process itself and their willingness to use it when so many concede that "when you revise, you are forced to think in ways you did not before." Regarding revision, students fell into two distinct factions: those who saw revision as correcting or fixing mistakes versus those who saw it as rewriting, rethinking, re*see*ing their writing and ideas. Of course, students' willingness to enter into a writing process to its full capacity depends on their past experiences with such processes and how engaged they are, something we must consider when deciding up front what we want them to write and how we want them to write about it.

Again, each academic writing assignment is akin to a journey, our students both travelers and users of all the maps and means (i.e., the assignments and the handouts on which they are explained) we give them. So, too, are journeys fraught with inevitable problems, which we must anticipate and either remove or reframe in such a way that the problems become baked into the assignment. We can transform such obstacles into opportunities to learn or improve their writing by making them part of the assignment, so that the assignment itself teaches students how to identify their own limits and work to overcome them. As they unfold, such process assignments can develop the independence and agility, confidence and knowledge of craft our students need to complete this and all future journeys.

The Forms and Features of Process Paper Assignments

As I mentioned at the beginning of this chapter, most of the six different types of writing assignments can be designed to include some or all of the elements of a writing-process approach. So the real question is: Which assignments should go through the full writing process? We should, after all, be sure that such assignments accomplish something more than a timed writing assignment would because, as Nancy Sommers observes, "responding to students' writing takes more time, thought, and energy than any other aspect of teaching" (2012). Whether we will respond, how, when, and why—these questions all demand our full consideration when we are designing the assignment and deciding whether to make it a process paper. So, too, do the means by which students will write: If we plan to have students write a process paper, we need to determine what tools and technology we want them to learn and use in the context of the assignment.

Though I integrate various strategies and steps in the writing process whenever my students write, the process assignments offer the greatest opportunity to teach students new or more advanced moves they'll need if they are to become more advanced readers, writers, and thinkers when they face academic writing assignments. In my class, this means designing and assigning academic papers of a certain length (two or more pages long), written with a certain purpose (to explain or argue), using certain techniques (structured note-taking while reading), and integrating technology throughout the writing process (Google Docs, Google Keep, Turnitin). Such papers are typically written about one or more texts that reward closer reading and make greater demands on students as writers than they can effectively manage on their own at this stage in their development. In other words, process papers, are, by design, more intentional and ambitious than other writing assignments because we are trying to accomplish so much through them. Here are a few representative examples of such assignments, each of which meets the criteria just listed, to give you a sense of the forms such writing tasks take in my class:

- ▶ *Literary Analysis:* Analyze one or more literary texts and the authors' treatment of a topic or literary element, such as imagery or theme, over the course of the text(s). My colleagues, for example, have students do a "concept trace" when reading *Macbeth* in which students examine how Shakespeare's use of a specific word (e.g., *blood*) shifts throughout the text. In *Reading Like a Writer*, Francine Prose recounts the experience in high school of being told to "go through the two tragedies [*Oedipus Rex* and *King Lear*] and circle every reference to eyes, light, darkness, and vision, then draw some conclusion on which we could base our final essay," an experience she describes as "learning to read in a whole new way" (2006, 4).

- ▶ *Structural Approach:* Apply a structured model or pattern such as the hero's journey (when reading *The Odyssey*) or French and Raven's (1959) six bases of power model (when reading, for example, *1984*). This approach requires setting up the way you want students to read and the tools or techniques they will use before you ever introduce the assignment. You are, in other words, giving students a structure and a strategy they can use to direct their attention, to both generate and sift ideas and examples as they read and, eventually, write. Additional examples of such structures you could provide for them to use for their papers would be *Investor's Business Daily's* "Ten Secrets to Success" or Abraham Maslow's hierarchy of human needs. Models such as these create a conversation between the texts you are considering by providing a structure you can map the primary text onto. If I were using Maslow's hierarchy to examine *Into the Wild*, for example, it would allow me to discuss Christopher McCandless' efforts to meet his different needs as detailed in the book.

- ▶ *Critical Theory or Rhetorical Analysis:* Examine one or more texts through the lens of critical theory or rhetoric. In such an assignment, students choose up front which critical lens, for example, they wish to apply to their reading. Whether they are reading the work(s) through the lens of feminist or Marxist theory, postcolonial or postmodern theory, the purpose is the same: to direct their attention and develop their ability first to read and then to write about specific ideas and how authors treat them. When it comes to reading rhetorically to analyze an author's argument, look to the case study of how my students read and write about Jon Krakauer's *Into the Wild* in the section that follows.

What do these representative examples have in common? They all assume that any academic writing assignment will be grounded in the act of reading and writing about text. Each one emphasizes the fundamental importance of integrating the reading, writing, and thinking in a coherent, effective way that engages students while also improving their essential academic literacies and preparing them for college-level academic writing. This integrated approach is summed up here by Bill Robinson, my mentor teacher in composition, in a brief article he wrote about the approach he worked so hard to teach those of us who were lucky enough to study under him at San Francisco State University:

> Students must write on assignments that require them to use what they've read. Only in that way will they start learning to read with accuracy and comprehension. Such assignments, if well designed, should also bring the world . . . into the . . . writing classroom, where it surely belongs. (n.d.)

Robinson goes on to describe his own classroom, an experience I witnessed often, focusing on the process by which students generated and refined their ideas for an essay they were writing, one that required them to draw on different readings about how societies are organized:

> Students' conclusions [from the readings and subsequent discussions about them] were insightful and perceptive. Next, they will bring trial outlines of their papers, and we will put them on the board and critique them, shooting for papers that will progress in an orderly and logical way to whatever conclusion each student wants to come to. After that, they will bring in rough drafts for peer review, using criteria sheets provided, the focus again on organization and content. (They work on their sentence skills through sentence-combining and their errors through individual exercises.) These students have read adult texts and understood them. Now they will create their own, using a combination of what they've learned and their own insights. They will also have advanced both their reading and their writing skills. And that's what I am aiming for.

The process Robinson describes is far from fixed; there is no one way to approach a process paper or writing as a process. My own approach to the process itself complements the more traditional version Robinson describes but focuses a bit more on the moves and skills we want students to learn and internalize as academic readers, thinkers, and writers:

▶ *generating and gathering* ideas, information, connections, and topics by reading, discussing, researching, and writing

▶ *sorting and selecting* the best and most relevant sources, examples, details, and ideas

FIGURE 4–1 I often gather quotations about a topic or provide the "Commonplace Book" pages from the *American Scholar*, which collects quotations around a theme, to help kids generate ideas about a topic.

FIGURE 4–2 Julianne and Monique read and respond to a text in order to come up with ideas for the papers they will eventually write.

FIGURE 4–3 Drew and Uma read through the different ideas, capturing those that seem useful for helping them come up with ideas for the paper they must write about *Crime and Punishment*. We might compare this approach to a low-tech form of crowdsourcing of writing ideas.

FIGURE 4–4 Vinny and Keone, along with their other group members, use the orientation–disorientation–new orientation model to generate ideas for their essay about *Siddhartha*.

- *designing and drafting* the paper in its early stages, including organizational structures, initial efforts at layout, figures, images, or other content as appropriate to the assignment's purpose

- *refining and revising* the paper as a result of new insights gained through subsequent discussions, additional reading, or response from peers and teacher

- *evaluating and editing* the paper to determine if it satisfies all the requirements of the assignment and making specific changes to address such needs as clarity, coherence, correctness, concision, and conventions of genre (This is a point at which we might make more deliberate use of applications such as Turnitin's Revision Assistant or Grammarly.)

- *proofreading and presenting*, which comes at the end, giving the student writer one last chance to find and fix any last-minute errors before presenting the finished paper to the teacher or other audience

- *reviewing and reflecting*, which involve metacognitive processes aimed at reviewing what tools or techniques did or did not work this time around and reflecting, based on the review, on how the student can apply these lessons to the next paper he or she writes.

Prior to ever giving students the handout that details which of these stages in the writing process an assignment will include (see Figures 4–1 through 4–4), I have to decide where, when, how, and why we should incorporate technology. Various apps offer help with different steps in the process; some (Google Docs, Google Keep, NoodleTools) are more efficient and effective than others. I remain a minimalist when it comes to the use of such apps, many of which become an unnecessary friction point in the writing process if they require time to learn how to use them that could be better spent writing and using the available features within Google Docs. Feedback plays a crucial role throughout the process, of course (see Figures 4–5 through 4–7). In my class, such feedback can come through peer response, individual conferences with me, a checklist, or the rubric I provide them before they begin writing. Feedback also comes in a more automated form from the GradeMark or Revision Assistant features of Turnitin.

Throughout the writing process, I also provide targeted feedback through minilessons in which I focus, for example, on how, when, and why to integrate evidence or ideas from the text(s) they read, if that is

FIGURE 4–5 This is a screenshot of the Voice Memos app I use on my iPhone to record and send to students my feedback on their papers. After recording the feedback, I click the Send icon and it goes directly to the student's email inbox.

FIGURE 4–6 The students go through their papers with headphones on, listening to my feedback about their papers and making lists of what they need to do when revising their papers before resubmitting.

FIGURE 4–7 After the students get my audio feedback, they can meet with me during class for individualized help about my feedback or how to implement the suggestions. Here, Hanna Piña and I confer about her paper, working directly from the screen of her laptop.

a common problem I have observed in my conversations with them about their papers. During such lessons, I often use the high school edition of *They Say/I Say: The Moves That Matter in Academic Writing* (Graff and Birkenstein 2014). In most cases, I provide detailed, formal feedback on process papers through audio notes using the Voice Memos app on my iPhone or the voice feedback feature within Turnitin. This approach allows me to give students detailed, personal feedback, which they then listen to in class and use to create a to-do list when returning to revise their papers after they thought they were finished.

Do I go back and reread all those papers after they have made these revisions? Of course not! I tell them I will simply look at the revision history in Google Docs, and if it provides evidence of all their hard work to revise, the grade will go up a full grade; if it does not, it will go down a grade; if it shows some effort to improve the paper, the grade will remain the same. As the case study that appears in the next section shows, students find this process engaging and helpful (see Figure 4–8).

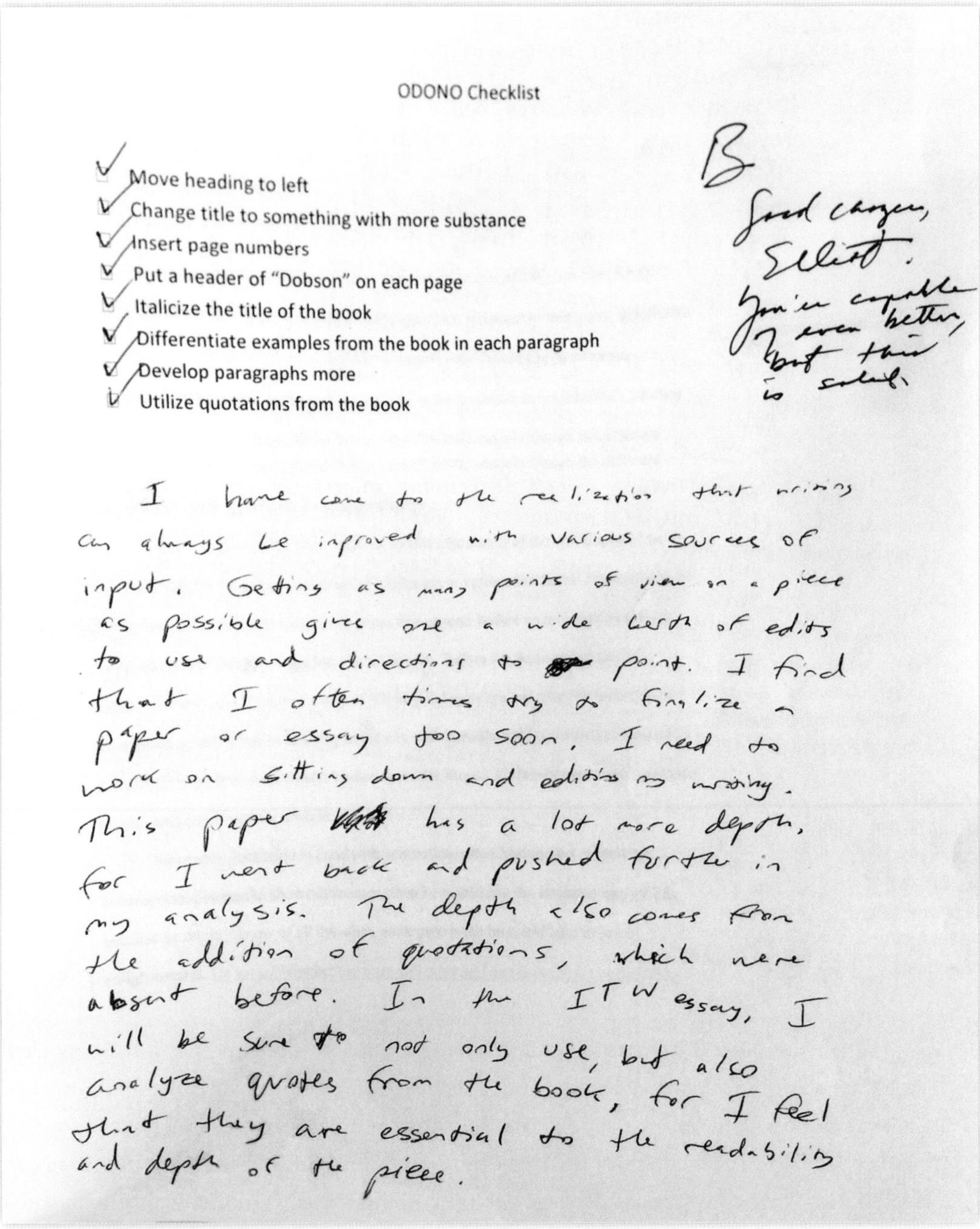

ODONO Checklist

- ✓ Move heading to left
- ✓ Change title to something with more substance
- ✓ Insert page numbers
- ✓ Put a header of "Dobson" on each page
- ✓ Italicize the title of the book
- ✓ Differentiate examples from the book in each paragraph
- ✓ Develop paragraphs more
- ✓ Utilize quotations from the book

B

Good changes, Elliot.

You're capable of even better, but this is solid.

I have come to the realization that writing can always be improved with various sources of input. Getting as many points of view on a piece as possible gives one a wide berth of edits to use and directions to point. I find that I often times try to finalize a paper or essay too soon. I need to work on sitting down and editing my writing. This paper has a lot more depth, for I went back and pushed further in my analysis. The depth also comes from the addition of quotations, which were absent before. In the ITW essay, I will be sure to not only use, but also analyze quotes from the book, for I feel that they are essential to the readability and depth of the piece.

FIGURE 4–8 Sample of a checklist Elliot created in response to audio feedback and his subsequent reflection on the cycle of feedback on and revision of his writing

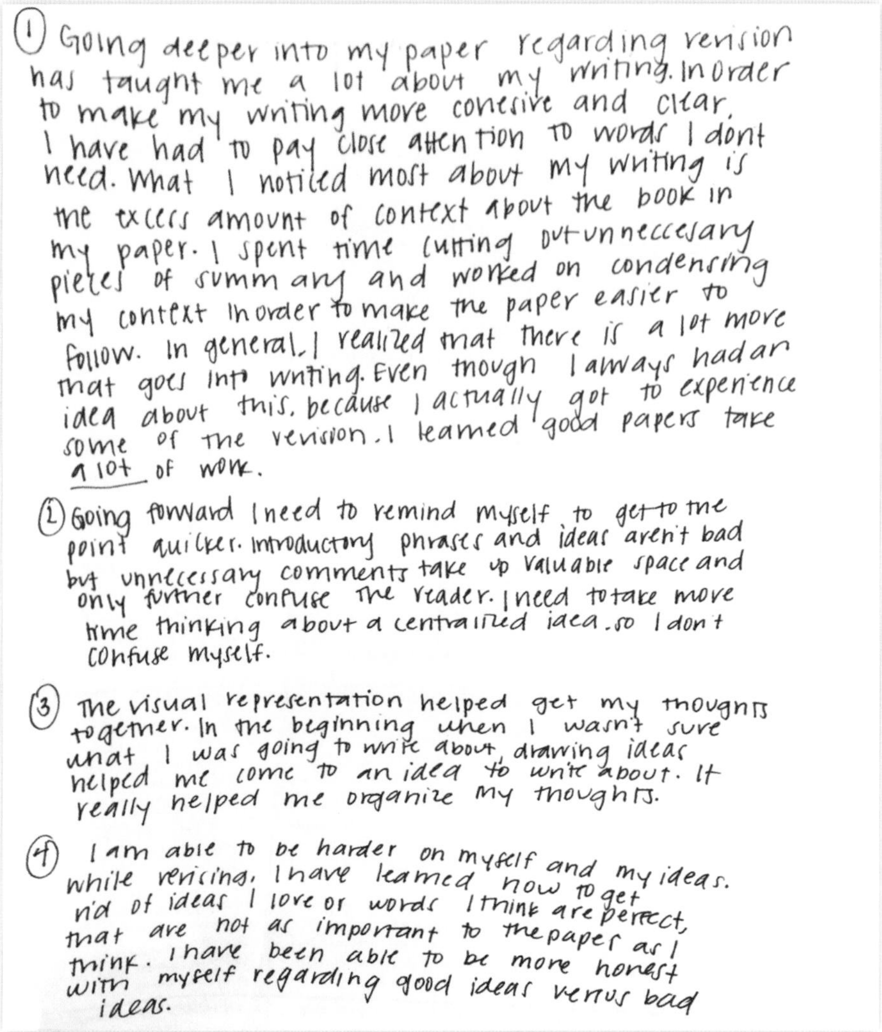

① Going deeper into my paper regarding revision has taught me a lot about my writing. In order to make my writing more cohesive and clear, I have had to pay close attention to words I dont need. What I noticed most about my writing is the excess amount of context about the book in my paper. I spent time cutting out unneccesary pieces of summary and worked on condensing my context in order to make the paper easier to follow. In general, I realized that there is a lot more that goes into writing. Even though I always had an idea about this, because I actually got to experience some of the revision, I learned good papers take a lot of work.

② Going forward I need to remind myself to get to the point quicker. Introductory phrases and ideas aren't bad but unnecessary comments take up valuable space and only further confuse the reader. I need to take more time thinking about a centralized idea, so I don't confuse myself.

③ The visual representation helped get my thoughts together. In the beginning when I wasn't sure what I was going to write about, drawing ideas helped me come to an idea to write about. It really helped me organize my thoughts.

④ I am able to be harder on myself and my ideas. while revising, I have learned how to get rid of ideas I love or words I think are perfect, that are not as important to the paper as I think. I have been able to be more honest with myself regarding good ideas versus bad ideas.

FIGURE 4–9 Senior Lindsey reflects on her overall performance and process on a finished paper and considers the implications for future writing assignments.

When the process has run its course, the last thing to do, time permitting, is have students reflect on what they learned about their writing through this paper and how they can use those lessons on the next paper to improve their performance (see Figure 4–9). To this end, I have students write a final reflection both for themselves and for me so we can both know what each student needs to focus on going forward. I usually give them some generic suggestions to guide their reflections: Thoughts about how you approached the writing of the paper? What do you need to remember to do on future papers based on your experience with this one? What strategies, tools, or techniques worked; which ones didn't? Why? Any final thoughts about your performance, process, or progress here as a writer?

Classroom Connection: What Process Paper Assignments Look Like in My Class

The following case study process assignment focuses on Jon Krakauer's nonfiction book *Into the Wild*, though I have used this same method with numerous other process papers when we were reading and writing about a book or collection of shorter texts from a reader such as *Uncharted Territory: A High School Reader* (Burke 2017a). Because I teach seniors, the reading and writing assignment focuses on the arguments Krakauer makes about the transition from adolescence to adulthood, specifically as related to his subject's quest for freedom from his past and society.

When designing such a process writing assignment for any book or unit, I begin by asking what conversations about the text(s) we are required to teach will engage my students the most. However, such texts and conversations must not only engage but also challenge students to read, write, and think in new or more demanding ways than previous assignments. Since I teach seniors, I feel compelled to ensure that the assignment cultivates their independence as readers and writers while making available the support some still need through templates, models, or strategies they can use when reading or writing about the assigned texts. At this point in the design process, it is also important that I identify those skills for which this assignment would create a context for students to learn or improve while maintaining the emphasis on engagement that is so essential to students' success in my class and beyond (see Figure 4–10).

In designing the actual handout for the writing assignment itself, I frame all the above within the "Overview" section of the document, where I sum up what they will do and why. This allows me to develop and examine my rationale for the assignment and articulate it for the ones who will *use* the assignment: my students. The first part of the assignment then appears at the top of the assignment sheet:

Into the Wild: An Inquiry into Freedom

Mr. Burke/English 4

Overview

We will read *Into the Wild* as an inquiry into the concept of freedom. To that end, we will consider a range of perspectives (Adler, Thoreau, Maslow); definitions (*liberty, freedom, license, autonomous, independent*); and approaches (philosophical, psychological, socioeconomic). For this assignment, you will examine that aspect or view of freedom that interests you most and reveals your understanding of Krakauer's ideas, his book, and its hero, Christopher McCandless.

Into the Wild: An Inquiry into Freedom
Mr. Burke/English 4

Overview We will read *Into the Wild* as an inquiry into the concept of freedom. To that end, we will consider a range of perspectives (Adler, Thoreau, Maslow); definitions (*liberty*, *freedom*, *license*, *autonomous*, *independent*); and approaches (philosophical, psychological, socioeconomic). For this assignment, you will examine that aspect or view of freedom that interests you most and reveals your understanding of Krakauer's ideas, his book, and its hero, Christopher McCandless.

Objectives This assignment is designed to teach you how or improve your ability to

- ► make a strong claim about the meaning or importance of a text that you can support with reasoning and evidence from the text(s) you analyze
- ► read a literary or nonfiction text for the arguments its author tries to make
- ► draft, revise, and edit your paper for cogency and correctness

Directions You will write a draft of this paper as you read *Into the Wild* by

- ☐ reading each chapter to discover what Krakauer or McCandless says about freedom
- ☐ making a claim about what Krakauer or McCandless says about freedom, providing the reasoning and evidence from the chapter to support your claim
- ☐ discussing your claims for each chapter to improve your understanding of the text and help you gather ideas for writing
- ☐ writing a draft of a paragraph for each chapter using your notes and ideas from the discussion in an academic style appropriate to the task and topic
- ☐ organizing your selected draft paragraphs into a logical sequence as body paragraphs for an essay about Krakauer's treatment of freedom in *Into the Wild*
- ☐ writing an effective introduction and conclusion that fit with your body paragraphs
- ☐ revising and editing your draft for clarity, cohesion, and correctness

Guidelines This paper should

- ☐ have 6 paragraphs: 1 introduction, 1 conclusion, and 4 paragraphs written in response to *Into the Wild* as we read it (all of which should be related to the same idea)
- ☐ be double-spaced, use 1-inch margins and a 12-point font, and be formatted in a serif font (use Cambria, not Calibri, which is a **sans serif** font), with a header formatted with the page number and your name in the upper-right corner
- ☐ include textual evidence in the form of direct and indirect quotations, each one properly cited in the text (according to the *BHS MLA 8th Edition Style Guide*)
- ☐ display your name, my name, the period, and the class on first page, left-justified

Assessment This paper will be evaluated using the attached rubric for argument papers.

FIGURE 4–10 Note the use of check boxes in such handouts as a way to help students keep track of what they have done and need to do; also, take note of the verbs that begin each item, as these are ways to make sure the cognitive demands are adequate.

Having determined that this paper about *Into the Wild* will be a process paper, I then turn my attention to the objectives of this assignment. Here, we encounter the first of many such crossroads throughout the process-assignment design process, for every teacher works within a different culture and set of constraints in his or her school and department. Some of us work in schools where we are required to state the specific standards this writing assignment addresses and assesses; others, however, may be required or simply prefer to identify the objectives of the assignment in more student-friendly language. After experimenting with this feature of the assignment, I have concluded that it is best to identify the objectives as one would enter the GPS coordinates before setting out on a trip and to write those objectives in language that is clear, accessible, and useful. Kids do not care about standards, though they do want to know that you know where you are going and why and that you have a good plan to help them get there. Also, given that you could usually list nearly all of the state ELA standards for every process paper, it is best to limit it to a few important, teachable statements. For the *Into the Wild* assignment, the assignment sheet features the following objectives, just after the "Overview" section:

Objectives

This assignment is designed to teach you how or improve your ability to

- ▶ make a strong claim about the meaning or importance of a text that you can support with reasoning and evidence from the text(s) you analyze
- ▶ read a literary or nonfiction text for the arguments its author tries to make
- ▶ draft, revise, and edit your paper for cogency and correctness

These three objectives identify a manageable set of tasks appropriate to the paper; also, they help my colleagues and me prioritize, for students and ourselves, what we should teach and what we will try to accomplish through this particular process assignment. If we list more, it is for the administrator who might be evaluating or observing us, not for the kids. We also run the risk of turning our assignment into the instructional equivalent of a turducken that feeds all but nourishes none.

Though we might list only these few key objectives, we must stop to acknowledge that there are other standards and expectations we might want to address through this assignment. As we list our objectives and before we advance to the heart of the assignment—the directions for the writing task itself—we should ask ourselves, for example, what technology standards we can incorporate (without having to spell them out for students) into the assignment. At this point, we should also ask if the assignment meets the needs for equity and access for our English learners or students with special needs and whether it is culturally responsive and engaging. If you are teaching an AP or honors class, this would be the moment to ask how appropriate these objectives and the subsequent tasks are for your class in light of its purposes and students' potential.

Academic
Essentials
Overview

Other, more personal goals come into play here for some teachers, depending on the kids and the context in which you teach: soft skills, critical thinking, workplace skills, and a range of related academic literacies that can be taught or improved through this assignment (see the Academic Essentials Overview). Now is the time, in other words, to acknowledge to ourselves what we value and intend to convey to and, for some, inculcate into our students through this assignment. This can be the point where such complex issues as our own biases arise, as well as more controversial ideas such as safe spaces or the potential of an assignment to trigger or otherwise upset some students.

Having created the overview, which allows me to provide the rationale for the assignment and frame it in some larger context, and identified the objectives, which show the students that we at least have some rationale for our demands on their precious time, I now come to the "Directions" section, which spells out for students what they must do:

Directions

You will write a draft of this paper as you read *Into the Wild* by

- ☐ reading each chapter to discover what Krakauer or McCandless says about freedom
- ☐ making a claim about what they say about freedom, providing the reasoning and evidence from the chapter to support your claim
- ☐ discussing your claims for each chapter to improve your understanding of the text and help you gather ideas for writing
- ☐ writing a draft of a paragraph for each chapter using your notes and ideas from the discussion in an academic style appropriate to the task and topic
- ☐ organizing your selected draft paragraphs into a logical sequence as body paragraphs for an essay about Krakauer's treatment of freedom in *Into the Wild*
- ☐ writing an effective introduction and conclusion that fit with your body paragraphs
- ☐ revising and editing your draft for clarity, cohesion, and correctness

The idea in these directions is to think all the way through the assignment, starting with the verbs that capture the academic and cognitive moves I want my students to learn or improve (see Figure 4–11). In crafting the directions, I deliberately emphasize the skills they need to use and that I can teach as we move through the writing process. Such a checklist serves an equally important purpose of providing feedback, since students can regularly consult it to evaluate their progress on the assignment and the degree to which they are satisfying the assignment's requirements. Embedded within these directions are also the elements I will assess. Whereas the "Objectives" section uses bullets for its list,

The A-LIST: Essential Academic Words

1	Analyze	break something down methodically into its parts break **down • deconstruct • examine**
2	Argue	provide reasons or evidence to support or oppose **claim • persuade • propose**
3	Compare/Contrast	identify similarities or differences between items **delineate • differentiate • distinguish**
4	Describe	report what one observes or does **illustrate • report • represent**
5	Determine	make a decision or arrive at a conclusion after considering all possible options, perspectives, or results **establish • identify • define**
6	Develop	improve the quality or substance of **formulate • generate • elaborate**
7	Evaluate	establish value, amount, importance, or effectiveness **assess • figure out • gauge**
8	Explain	provide reasons for what happened or one's actions **clarify • demonstrate • discuss**
9	Imagine	create a picture in one's mind; speculate or predict **anticipate • hypothesize • predict**
10	Integrate	make whole by combining the different parts into one **combine • incorporate • synthesize**
11	Interpret	draw from a text or data set some meaning or significance **deduce • infer • translate**
12	Organize	arrange or put in order **arrange • classify • form**
13	Summarize	retell the essential details of what happened **outline • paraphrase • report**
14	Support	offer evidence or data to illustrate your point **cite • justify • maintain**
15	Transform	change in form, function, or nature to reveal or emphasize **alter • change • convert**

FIGURE 4–11 List of essential academic words

the "Directions" section uses check boxes. The difference and reasoning is simple: A check box signals what students must do (and thus should be able to check off), whereas a bullet indicates the information students must know or use.

Finally, we come to the last two sections in the writing assignment template: "Guidelines" and "Assessment." Again, as with the "Directions" items, the "Guidelines" section requires me to think through the entire assignment and identify those smaller aspects of writing that students need to learn or improve. For example, in the "Guidelines" section included in this assignment, I specifically required them to have six paragraphs as a deliberately incremental step away from the five-paragraph formula they were still clinging to at that point in the year; otherwise, I never specify the number of paragraphs in an assignment. Also, because document design is a legitimate and increasingly important part of writing in the real world, I always make specific but reasonable demands in this area so they can learn, in this case, about the differences between serif and sans serif fonts and the way to insert and format headers, skills that some but not all students know when they enter my class in August. Here is the "Guidelines" section from the *Into the Wild* process assignment:

Guidelines

This paper should

- ☐ have 6 paragraphs: 1 introduction, 1 conclusion, and 4 paragraphs written in response to *Into the Wild* as we read it (all of which should be related to the same idea)
- ☐ be double-spaced, use 1-inch margins and a 12-point font, and be formatted in a serif font (use Cambria not Calibri, which is a **sans serif** font), with a header formatted with the page number and your name in the upper-right corner)
- ☐ include textual evidence in the form of direct and indirect quotations, each one properly cited in the text (according to the *BHS MLA 8th Edition Style Guide*)
- ☐ display your name, my name, the period, and the class on first page, left-justified

As for the "Assessment" section included at the bottom of the assignment, it serves to direct students to the Argument Rubric, which I developed for our department for academic argument papers so that the criteria would be clear and consistent across assignments and teachers.

Argument
Writing Rubric

Assessment

This paper will be evaluated using the attached rubric for argument papers.

It is important to emphasize that feedback is occurring by multiple means at junctures throughout the entire process. It comes, first, from the handout I just finished describing in detail, which is designed to be used as a checklist, a guide, and a means of feedback about where a student is in the process of composing the paper at any point. Additional sources of feedback throughout the process include peer response, group discussions of ideas, and drafts. My own role changes throughout the process. I offer guided feedback to the full class in response to struggles I observe to be common to all students at different points in the process. At other points, I give them annotated models on paper or a guided tour of a model projected from my iPad so that I can mark it up to draw their attention to those items more relevant to their current stage in the composing process. On the more individual level, I meet with students at their desks, in their groups, or separately at my desk so we can take a deeper dive to discuss their writing. As they move into the editing process, several digital resources help students identify conventions and usage errors, such as Grammarly and Turnitin, which students use to fix those errors hard to spot at that stage. Finally, I provide feedback when the paper is submitted using either the voice recorder in Turnitin's Revision Assistant or the Voice Memos app on my iPhone, which allows me to give up to seven minutes of feedback before sending it as an attachment in an email. As I mentioned earlier, they then use that feedback for one last round of revision before submitting the paper for a final grade.

The preceding explanation of the design of the *Into the Wild* process paper assignment may leave you wondering what exactly it looks like in action with real students. When designing the experience of a process assignment such as this, I am always trying to incorporate into the reading experience those academic essentials they need to work on, but without, I hope, turning the book into an exercise book that ruins their experience as readers and, in the long run, makes them hate reading.

With these challenges in mind, the demands I made for reading *Into the Wild* and writing the draft of the paper were simple: Read each chapter with the idea of freedom in mind, looking for whatever point author Jon Krakauer or Christopher McCandless, the hero of Krakauer's story, makes about freedom. As this writing assignment came early in the year as part of our *Into the Wild* unit, and reading book-length nonfiction was new to many of my students, I provided them with the initial claims I had developed while reading the first six chapters ahead of time. This meant that they read with my claims in mind to find supporting evidence in the form of three quotations from the text, which they were to jot down, along with page citations. My primary rationale for this first stage was to limit the cognitive load of the assignment while also setting the standard for what I expected. By giving them a working claim to use when reading, I prevented them, initially, from having to read, analyze the text, and generate a claim about what it said about freedom. The focus here was on reading for the evidence to support such claims. By taking this initial time to calibrate their attention and set their criteria for how to read and what to read for, I laid a foundation for what became a successful unit and paper. Once you start analyzing your assignments, you will often be amazed to realize how many discrete cognitive moves, many of them very complex, you were asking students to make; suddenly you realize why so many struggled with the assignment or simply chose not to do it at all.

After sending students home with my claim for the first chapter and the assignment to finish the chapter, they returned the next day, with my claim and their three quotations, and entered into small-group discussions to revise and refine their ideas, after which they used all they had to write a draft of a paragraph using my claim (see Figures 4–12 and 4–13). Here are the claims I gave them for the first two chapters:

1. **Claim:** The first impression one gets of Chris McCandless is that he wants to escape mainstream American society in general and his own past and family in particular.

2. **Claim:** Alaska is a breathtaking but inhospitable landscape that resists man's best efforts to control it—and the government's attempts to control the people who live there.

Raquel provides a representative example of what this process looked like; her example comes from Chapter 5 of *Into the Wild*:

Chapter 5 Claim: One thing we can never get entirely free of or fully escape is our need for money.

Chapter 5 Quotes
- "... he was holding down a fulltime job, flipping Quarter Pounders at a McDonald's on the main drag. . . . Outwardly, he was living a surprisingly conventional existence, even going so far as to open a saving account at a local bank" (39).
- "[Chris'd] get moody, wouldn't like to be bothered. Seemed like a kid who was looking for something, looking for *something*, just didn't know what it was. I was like that once, but then I realized what I was looking for: Money! Ha! Ha hyah, hooh boy!" (42).
- "Man, you gotta have money to get along in this world" (46).

Using the claim I provided and the quotations she gathered as she read Chapter 5, Raquel then came into class to discuss the claim, the chapter, and her quotations with the members of her group. The aim here was to generate and gather new ideas and deepen her

FIGURE 4–12 Students begin the class by getting into groups to discuss the chapter, the claim, and the quotations they gathered in support of it. These discussions are meant to prepare them to write the paragraph in which they will develop the claim for that chapter of *Into the Wild*.

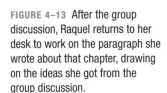

FIGURE 4–13 After the group discussion, Raquel returns to her desk to work on the paragraph she wrote about that chapter, drawing on the ideas she got from the group discussion.

own through the give-and-take of the discussion. When they were finished, Raquel wrote the draft paragraph for that chapter:

Chapter 5 *Into the Wild* Paragraph

One thing we can never get entirely free of or fully escape is our need for money. Chris McCandless tried to live without money but was told that ". . . you gotta have money to get along in this world" (46) and so I think that he was experiencing this first hand. As a result, he decided to ". . . [hold] down a fulltime job, flipping Quarter Pounders at a McDonald's on the main drag. . . . Outwardly, he was living a surprisingly conventional existence, even going so far as to open a saving account at a local bank" (39). Some might argue that money cannot buy happiness; however, I believe that it does, to some extent. As sadistic as this might sound, money does control our society. Sometimes, it is one's financial instability that does not allow one to be completely free. For example, many seniors are deciding where to go to college, but some may not be able to attend certain colleges because their families do not have the financial stability to support them and they are unwilling to take out loans. Others might want to move out and take a gap year, but in order to move out, they need money. My point is, one's freedom is limited and directly varies according to one's situation. In this respect, McCandless is free to live out his dream because he comes from a family with money and knows he is always free to return home.

As I said, this was a draft paragraph, so if Raquel eventually chose to include it in her essay when we finished *Into the Wild*, she would have to go through the full process of revision, editing for clarity and correctness. Right now, however, we were generating ideas and drafting the parts that would later be sorted and assembled into a whole. It is worth mentioning that Raquel came from a single-parent family and was to be the first in her family to attend college. That their small apartment was, at the time, crowded with a family of newly arrived relatives from Central America who did not have the money to get their own place that year only makes Raquel's remarks and her own views on freedom more poignant.

This reading-and-composing cycle repeated itself with each of the first six chapters, at which point their mastery of supporting and developing my claims suggested they were ready to develop their own claims for which they would also find supporting evidence. As a transition, I provided them with a set of quotations from Chapter 7 from which they were to draw supporting evidence for the claim they developed. I did this to maintain a level of challenge and quality control. So from Chapter 8 on, students came in with a working claim about some aspect of freedom from that next chapter and evidence to support it, all of which they used to have the same generative conversations in small groups before writing the next draft of the paragraph.

As a result of this recursive read–discuss–write cycle, which began in class and continued at home each night, students worked to meet the goals of the assignment while reading for academic purposes about a subject that, as seniors, they found meaningful and important. By the time they finished the book, they had become adept at reading rhetorically and using the discussion to prepare them to write and thus had a full set of paragraphs to choose from when selecting the four body paragraphs they'd use to construct their complete draft of their essay. They then wrote an introduction and a conclusion and revised the paper through a series of directed processes that included peer review before submitting it (see Figures 4–14 through 4–17). After listening to and considering my feedback, in the form of audio comments, they revised one more time before we considered the assignment done. Michael, a student in my senior class, had the following comments about how we used the audio feedback in my class:

> I didn't dread revising this paper as much as I normally do. I found it really helpful to have the voice memo feedback telling me what to improve on. If I had been left to revise without it, I probably wouldn't have changed much. I also liked the grammar corrections that Turnitin suggested. In the past, I did not revise my papers that much. Once I finished writing them and going through it that first time, I never felt like I had anything to change. That's why I like getting this audio and grammar feedback, because it gives me specific things to revise that I might not have noticed or known to do on my own. Specifically, Mr. Burke pointed out that I didn't discuss what some of the quotations meant or why they mattered. This observation prompted me to go back and develop that part of the paper. It will also make me more aware of doing this in the future when writing other papers. I will now pay more attention to using the "says-means-matters" and the "So what?" "Who cares?" strategies when writing and revising.

At several points throughout the process of reading and writing about *Into the Wild*, during which we also read shorter nonfiction works, including an excerpt from *Walden*, I distributed index cards and asked students to provide feedback about the reading–discussing–writing process we were using, how cognitively demanding and engaging it was, and whether it was, on the whole, helping them to comprehend the book and other readings better. Luke wrote the following:

> I haven't experienced an English class that requires so much effort. Although difficult at first, it is easy enough once you get the hang of the process. I am thankful that this class is giving us a small taste of what college English will be like. As for the process itself, the cycle definitely helps me get a deeper understanding of the text, especially when reading with a question in mind. I found it difficult at first to create a claim for chapters 9 and 10 because I read them at first without a question in mind. The discussions we have had and the claims and the book's meaning definitely help me in staying engaged in the book.

Throughout the process, feedback comes in many different forms. The handouts themselves, as shown earlier, offer guidelines and checklists students can consult through-out the writing process to see if their paper has what is required and does what it should. The discussion groups offer additional forms of feedback, early on about their ideas and later, once they are drafting and revising, on the ideas and the writing. In addition, I confer with them at their desk or more privately at my own desk up front at different junctures. Through minilessons about specific writing moves their papers should make,

FIGURE 4–14 Students such as Charlie prepare to provide minilessons to the class based on ideas from *They Say/I Say*, by Graff and Birkenstein (2014). These minilessons correspond with different aspects of the writing they are doing, in this case how to integrate quotations from sources.

CAN <u>YOU</u> OVERANALYZE A "QUOTATION ?"

- EXPLAIN quotations when they are long, complex, or confusing in nature.

- INTERPRET the author's point of view IN YOUR OWN WORDS,

- INCLUDE your opinion to provide substantial argument basis

~ there is such a thing as OVERANALYZING, but it is better to explain a quotation in excess rather than leave the reader confused.

FIGURE 4–15 An example of a complete poster students use to present their assigned content from *They Say/I Say*

FIGURE 4–16 Charlie begins the process of sorting through the many paragraphs he wrote while reading *Into the Wild* in order to select the paragraphs that he will use as body paragraphs in his essay.

FIGURE 4–17 Nick composes the complete draft of his essay, drawing from the book and the paragraphs he selected.

students also get feedback they can use to deepen their knowledge of the craft and improve the quality of this paper in particular.

Having gone through all those stages and done all that work, we arrive at a paper the students can submit with pride. Here is an abbreviated sample of Michael's essay about freedom from *Into the Wild*:

The Death of Freedom

Freedom as we know it is simply the power to do without restraint. Yet the problem is, it's not that simple. We, as humans, have created a puzzle out of freedom, adding so many layers that it is almost impossible to see where we started. In Jon Krakauer's book, *Into the Wild*, we meet Chris McCandless, a young man who attempts to solve this puzzle. Surrounded by contemporary American life, McCandless sets out to completely free himself in the Alaskan wilderness. However, what he doesn't know is that this power doesn't exist. Freedom in its purest form has expired.

The first form of freedom that Christopher McCandless tries to achieve is freedom from others. It seems simple enough. He is quick to abandon his human counterparts, "flitting out of their lives before anything is expected of him," but they refuse to let him go (Krakauer 55). After McCandless departs, his parents hire a private detective from the FBI to piece together his whereabouts. The other travelers McCandless befriends find themselves "attached to [him]" and writing to him frequently (Krakauer 55). And almost every person he speaks with tries to dissuade him from his grand adventure out of sheer concern. Slightly less obvious is the affection that McCandless feels for others. Despite his best attempts to avoid people, McCandless fails to suppress the emotion he feels when in the presence of others. According to Jan Burres, "He [has] a good time when he [is] around people, a real good time"

(Krakauer 44). Christopher McCandless is a social animal by nature, an innate programming that is impossible for him to shake.

After McCandless seemingly pushes everyone out of his life, he is still not free. As a citizen and inhabitant of the United States, McCandless is still subject to the law that governs the country. Although he is never caught, many things that McCandless does are illegal. He "[sneaks] into Mexico by paddling through open floodgates" (Krakauer 34). He trespasses into "U.S. Army's highly restricted Yuma Proving Ground" (Krakauer 33). The list goes on. And even though he never quite delves into the subject, when asked whether he has a hunting license McCandless scoffs, "How I feed myself is none of the government's business. Fuck their stupid rules" (Krakauer 6). Clearly, Christopher McCandless finds himself bound by the guidelines that govern us all. . . .

Freedom exists. It exists in some altered shape or form, to a certain degree or amount. But pure, unadulterated freedom can never be found. There will always be rules. There will always be obstacles. There will always be constraints. This is the world we have created for ourselves and this is the world Christopher McCandless found himself living in. He died trying to find freedom in its most unpolluted form, oblivious to its unrealistic terms. Yet the irony of it all is that on his incredible journey he might have stumbled upon the greatest, and closest to pure form of freedom there is: death.

A quick scan of the following abbreviated form of the Academic Writing Assignment Framework shows that this assignment meets these different criteria for an academic writing assignment. It engages students while also challenging them and improving their writing and other essential academic literacies in many ways that are

- ▶ anchored in clear goals linked to specific standards;
- ▶ grounded in texts that are engaging and demanding;
- ▶ cognitively demanding;
- ▶ emotionally and intellectually engaging to all students;
- ▶ designed to support students;
- ▶ assessed or evaluated according to criteria and requirements that are clearly stated; and
- ▶ written and formatted for maximum readability and ease of use.

Obstacles and Opportunities

I have tried to offer a glimpse into the experience of designing one process paper in my class. The process model outlined here, as well as the elements of the process paper assignment itself, differ little in my classes; that is, the assignments and process look pretty much the same whether I am teaching a freshman or senior class, an Advanced Placement or a college prep English class. What does sometimes differ, depending on the constraints of the class for which I design the assignment, is how long we have for a given assignment and the degree of support students need to meet the standards of the assignment. What can take a few weeks one year takes longer the next if, for example, I have a large number of special-needs students or the assignment gets disrupted by a string of holidays, PD days, or other intrusions we had not been able to anticipate.

One of the obstacles we all grapple with is time, especially on such an extended assignment as a process paper. Each stage of the assignment creates a rich opportunity to teach various elements of writing and strategies; however, one must maintain the momentum of the assignment or else it bogs down and becomes a death march. This same concern about momentum and engagement applies equally to reading: If we design an assignment that requires students to stop and smell every rose on every page in every chapter, students will quickly tire and turn to one of the many online sources that can help them pretend to have read the book. Far better to read, discuss, and write about it at a natural pace that moves toward a memorable finish and a well-written paper of which they can be proud.

Reflect on Your Own Practice

Take some time to consider the writing assignments I have discussed in this chapter under the category of process papers and compare them with your own classroom and curriculum. Specifically, I encourage you do to the following in your head, in writing, or as part of a discussion with members of your department or those instructional teams (sometimes called PLCs) to which you belong.

1. Generate a list of all the different process papers you have students do in a semester or during a specific unit you just finished or are about to begin. You might take a minute to examine the assumptions behind these different assignments to determine what qualifies them as process papers and how much of the writing process your students engage in during the different papers. Make notes as needed about ways you could improve your use or the design of process paper assignments based on your observations.

2. Examine the process paper assignments on the list you created or a smaller subset of representative assignments in light of the AWA Framework checklist provided on the previous page to assess the degree to which these writing assignments include or could be improved to better incorporate the features listed on the AWA Framework.

5 The Research Paper

Challenging Complexity

> *This paper was one of the most, if not the most, difficult papers I have ever had to write. I'm not whining or nagging, but I feel as though this was a reality check. I know that in college, I'll be given longer writing assignments with less time to write it and not nearly as much help as you provided. I don't want to drop out or fall behind.*
>
> —RAQUEL, former student reflecting on her ten-page Expert Project paper

The Research Paper: What It Is and Why We Assign It

My oldest son, Evan, sat at the dining room table reading a book by Jane Goodall for his anthropology class at the local city college, while my wife and I chatted quietly in the kitchen. Soon, however, we began to hear sounds of mounting frustration from the dining room. When I stuck my head in to ask if all was OK, Evan growled, "How am I supposed to write a ten-page paper about this damn book when I've already written three pages and have thirty-five more chapters to go?" I asked about the assignment, which he said called for him to summarize the book. After we looked over the assignment sheet, it was clear that he was not supposed to summarize the book but, rather, explain Jane Goodall's argument about human nature and how she arrived at it according to the book. Realizing that he did not have to summarize each chapter as he read it, Evan resumed reading and felt much more competent once he understood how he should be reading and what sort of information he would need later to write about Goodall's ideas.

By the time Evan and his brother, Whitman, graduated from college, they had written many papers, nearly all of them long, none of them about literature, and some of them (for Whitman, who studied business) in collaboration with others. One long paper Whitman wrote required him to research a company and interview one of its chief officers and then write up a ten-page analysis of the business and his research on it. Another paper, this one written with a few of his classmates, culminated in a thirty-page case study of a business (they chose Uber) that drew on their research from many sources and perspectives; the paper called for them to develop an argument, supported by their research, about why the particular business model was effective and what its potential weaknesses might be. My daughter, Nora, on the other hand, was in high school during the same years the boys were in college. In her AP language and composition course, which should have been equivalent to a college freshman composition course, Nora wrote only formulaic, timed practice essays in response to past AP prompts. No paper was ever longer than she could write in forty minutes, and she was asked to revise only to better meet the demands of the College Board scoring guide the teacher provided. Yes, she did well on the AP exam, but none of that prepared her as it should have for the demands of college writing the following year. A year later, Nora entered college, where one of her classes required four research papers written over the course of the semester.

Writing a major paper, which I will say is five pages (1,500 words) or longer, serves as a crucial stage in the formation of a student's intellectual and academic identity. Such papers make complex demands on both the teacher who designs the assignment and the students who must complete it. While there are many different types of major papers students might write in high school—the research paper, the term paper, the multigenre paper, the mixed-media or digital essay, the documentary report—I focus in this chapter on the research paper since this genre and all the skills related to it are emphasized in the standards of every state and essential to college success. The Common Core State Standards, as part of their writing standards, state that students will do the following:

Research to Build/Present Knowledge

1. Conduct short as well as more sustained research projects based on focused questions, demonstrating understanding of the subject under investigation.

2. Gather relevant information from multiple print and digital sources, assess the credibility and accuracy of each source, and integrate the information while avoiding plagiarism.

3. Draw evidence from literary or informational texts to support analysis, reflection, and research.

Range of Writing

4. Write routinely over extended time frames (time for research, reflection, and revision) and shorter time frames (a single sitting or a day or two) for a range of tasks, purposes, and audiences. (Burke 2013, 68)

Of the twenty-four states that opted out of the Common Core State Standards, twenty describe their state research requirements using the same words and also locate their standards for research in the writing section of their standards document. Only three states—Colorado, Missouri, and Virginia—place their research standards under their own separate heading. Texas, the only state whose standards depart completely from the other forty-nine states, has a separate research strand in its English language arts standards but is consistent with the other states, simply offering a more detailed description of what a research paper and all its related tasks involve. And both the International Baccalaureate (IB) "extended essay" (4,000 words) and the AP seminar course (two extended research papers that total nearly 4,000 words) make such research papers the culminating performance of their courses. Yet Applebee and Langer's study of writing in secondary schools throughout the United States found that most students are not writing anywhere near this much nor papers this long (2013). Only 12 percent of all the extended writing assignments they examined in their study were three pages or longer, the exception being those schools that had "a reputation for excellence in teaching writing," where 25 percent of the extended writing assignments were three or more pages. In addition, they noted that 40 percent of such extended writing took place in the twelfth-grade classes (30).

However, to graduate from high school having written nothing longer than three-page papers leaves those students most likely to struggle with limited hope for success in college. As Rebecca Cox notes in *College Fear Factor*, her book about first-year community college students, those "who are familiar with what is required and who are relatively confident from the start of their success as college students are most likely to achieve success. Conversely, those who are least conversant with the norms of higher education are at a distinct disadvantage; they are more likely to feel like outsiders and to doubt their ability to fit in" when they arrive at college (2009, 41). And they *will* write such long papers, for as Melzer found in his study of over 2,000 college writing assignments, "the research paper . . . is one of the most complex and dynamic genres in college writing and one that instructors assign as a tool to encourage students to think critically, to introduce them to ways of thinking in their discipline, and to prepare them for the workforce" (2014, 51).

What's more (and which has important implications for how we design such assignments), Andrea Lunsford and Karen Lunsford compared thousands of undergraduate papers and found that first-year students are asked to "write longer papers and are much more likely to be asked to write using sources than in the past, yet first year students cope with these assignments by shopping for bits of stuff that they assemble according to instructions" (Fister 2011). As the rest of this chapter will show, the inclination of students to skip the hard parts, combined with the challenge of writing the longer paper, presents important design considerations for us when we create major research assignments that can engage the three Hs—the head (intellect), heart (emotions), and hands (skills).

This idea of designing with the three Hs in mind highlights that college readiness is not the only aim of teaching the long paper. Nor is the major paper merely a convenient means of teaching a wide range of skills spelled out by your state's standards documents. At its best, the research paper provides an experience that is transformative, one that allows students to discover aspects of both themselves and their topic about which they were previously unaware, as Yvette, one of my students, writes when reflecting on her Expert Project paper:

> All in all my topic evolved throughout the year as has my view on the environment. I was able to really look into and form my viewpoint on the environment and how it has gone from a place we visit and explore, to being made of the digital devices and images of nature that surround us. I will continue to study the environment because it is something that is directly affecting our lives. The opportunity to read different articles and books, listen to TED Talks and survey people about my topic is one I will never forget. I had no idea there was so much to say about my topic or that I could actually write such a long paper. Ten pages! Now at dinner parties when the topic of the environment comes up, I am often one of the people leading the conversation. The experience of researching and writing about this topic over the course of the year is something I will always appreciate.

Throughout the remainder of this chapter, I focus primarily on the sort of research paper Yvette is reflecting on. However, when I taught AP literature, students wrote major papers about books (*Crime and Punishment, Hamlet, Frankenstein*), big questions and critical theories (What does it mean to be human?; postcolonial theory), and genres (poems, plays, short fiction, novels). Such major papers, generally around ten pages, were appropriate to the course; however, these more traditional literary analysis papers hold little appeal for most students not taking AP English. They do, however, challenge those more advanced students in necessary ways and serve to remind us that as our assignments should develop their ability not only to compose such papers but also to compose themselves.

What Students Say and How They Struggle with Research Papers

The aforementioned process of composing oneself, however, is rarely linear or easy, especially when we ask students to do something, such as write a ten-page research paper on a complex topic, they have not done before—or done at that level. They do not know what such a performance or paper looks like. Nor do they know that they can do it. Writing a major paper is a bit like the challenge of conducting an orchestra:

> There's no other requirement that demands the coordination and integration of so many different neurodevelopmental functions and academic subskills. Just think about it: writing requires you to generate good ideas, organize your thoughts, encode your ideas into clear language, remember many things at once (such as spelling, rules of punctuation, facts, and instructions), coordinate your fingers so they can keyboard or form letters, plan and monitor the quality of your work, and marshal the materials you need (pencils, reference books, or computer equipment) and your time. Writing also requires a great deal of concentration and mental effort. It takes energy and fortitude to complete a term paper. Intense focus is called for in answering an essay question well. All of those simultaneous demands must then be smoothly integrated and synchronized to achieve writing success. (Levine 2004, 6)

The Advanced Placement Capstone program offers a concise summary of the demands and struggles inherent in the research paper in the form of the acronym QUEST: **Q**uestion and Explore; **U**nderstand and Analyze; **E**valuate Multiple Perspectives; **S**ynthesize Ideas; **T**eam, Transform, and Transmit (see Figure 5–1). Not all students come into a class or begin a research paper disposed to "question and explore" a topic for an assignment that requires them to "challenge and expand the boundaries of [their] current knowledge" (College Board 2016, 6). Nor are all our students comfortable with being asked to "understand . . . analyze, [and] evaluate multiple perspectives"; yet the skills associated with these tasks are vital to one's adult success. The QUEST framework specifies that students need to learn to "contextualize arguments and comprehend authors' claims . . . [while also learning how to] consider individual perspectives and the larger conversation of varied points of view" (6). Though it is obvious to us that students, as apprentices to the academic enterprise, need to learn how to "entertain objections," "anticipate objections," and "name [their] naysayers" (Graff and Birkenstein 2014, 83), increased cultural tensions have made these thinking and writing moves as difficult to teach as they are important to learn. The QUEST framework wraps up its tour of the research paper process by asking students to "synthesize ideas" by combining "knowledge, ideas, and [their] own perspective into an argument" on which they can then "collaborate, reflect, and communicate . . . to their audience" (6).

Easier said than done, which is why we must provide ample time to help students identify and resolve those aspects of the research paper that challenge them most. Some challenges involve such factors as engagement, motivation, and commitment. In short, this means that students are challenged to find a topic they can grow into and stay with for a long period of time; in other words, longer papers require emotional, attentional, and intellectual stamina. Students also need to be able to generate—ideas, connections,

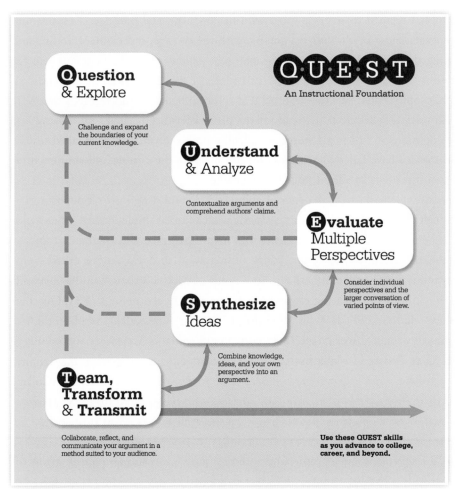

FIGURE 5–1
AP Capstone
QUEST diagram

questions—and persevere when their investigation into and efforts to convey their insights about their topic bog down or their motivation wanes. Students often have the sort of experience that Eliza described when she was a senior in my class:

> The Expert Project paper has been a very long process. I appreciate learning how to take critical notes on different sources, learning how to summarize and make connections between what we read. I now realize that I am not really that interested in media and social media anymore, though I am glad I was able to explore this topic. I probably would have changed my topic; however, that seemed too overwhelming to consider. Writing the big research paper was stressful because I struggled with deciding what to include and how not to repeat myself. I prefer to write shorter essays because they are concise and to the point.

While Eliza seemed to struggle more with her own internal processes—motivation, anxiety, engagement—other students grapple with the process, especially of finding and investigating the topic. Antonio, a young man who had a very difficult senior year for many reasons, confessed at the end of the first semester that he realized he had chosen a topic—philosophy—that was too esoteric; it was too difficult to find readings that were useful: "Almost every article that I read for the project has been a bust. All readings are someone's opinions . . . or just a summary of some philosophy. . . . I have failed to find a relevant topic. I have failed as a student for not meeting the criteria and your expectations. . . . At this point I realize I must find a new topic."

Others struggle with the experience of going so long and deep into a topic because it is so personal, the irony being that this is exactly what so many students love about major research experiences. While some students find investigating certain traumatic topics—sexual abuse, mental illness, addiction, gangs, immigration, and war, among others—empowering and transformative, others can hit a point of psychic exhaustion that makes it difficult to continue on with the research. Still, it is part of the process to explore their interests, experiences, and ideas; far more people feel like this student, whose topic was relationship abuse and whose paper, though only required to be ten pages, turned out to be a remarkable twenty-five-page examination of her topic:

> When I was first assigned the Expert Project and given the freedom to select any topic which I would like to research in detail, I immediately knew which topic to choose. But to be quite honest, I was expecting this to be just another English essay that I would struggle to write and probably get an average grade on. Except I didn't realize this assignment had the ability to impact me in the most personal way. As time progressed, my opinions started to surprise me. My opinions definitely altered as I delved deeper and deeper into my subject. Never in a million years would I have imagined myself to be so vocal about a topic which I mostly preferred to keep quiet about. When it was time to conclude my essay, what hit me was that I was able to learn so much about a topic yet also be able to openly express my own opinion and disagree with any statements which I did not believe in. Through this paper, I was given the platform to speak openly without facing judgement, which was all I ever wanted. In comparison to the other essays I had written during my 4 years of high school, the Expert Project paper helped me form my own solutions to problems I had within my life. The topic which I had the most difficulty speaking out about turned out to be a topic which I became passionate about thanks to the Expert Project.

The research paper, represented in this chapter by the Expert Project paper my students write, is designed to prepare students for the demands of college, a goal that others share and emphasize in their writings and work with students. Again, the skills and dispositions students need to cultivate are, for many, the same ones they most often struggle to master or even accept. Yet these different assignments discussed here and the struggles students face in completing them are embodied in the *Framework for Success in Postsecondary Writing*, which identifies the following "habits of mind" that its authors found to be crucial for success on the sort of extended academic writing we are talking about here. Note the implications for design as you read through them, for any good research paper assignment is going to incorporate these habits of mind and the related skills. This framework, created by the Council of Writing Program Administrators (CWPA), the National Council of Teachers of English (NCTE), and the National Writing Project (NWP), defines these habits of mind as "ways of approaching learning that are both intellectual and practical and that will support students' success in a variety of fields and disciplines . . . [by focusing on these] eight habits of mind essential for success in college writing":

- ▶ **Curiosity**—the desire to know more about the world.
- ▶ **Openness**—the willingness to consider new ways of being and thinking in the world.
- ▶ **Engagement**—a sense of investment and involvement in learning.
- ▶ **Creativity**—the ability to use novel approaches for generating, investigating, and representing ideas.
- ▶ **Persistence**—the ability to sustain interest in and attention to short- and long-term projects.
- ▶ **Responsibility**—the ability to take ownership of one's actions and understand the consequences of those actions for oneself and others.
- ▶ **Flexibility**—the ability to adapt to situations, expectations, or demands.
- ▶ **Metacognition**—the ability to reflect on one's own thinking as well as on the individual and cultural processes used to structure knowledge. (2011, 1)

In many ways, the idea of struggling on a major research paper is, to some degree, the point of designing and assigning such a paper. For a long paper of sound design will incorporate those experiences that help students to identify and overcome some of the most common problems with which the academic apprentice contends: management of time, attention, energy, resources, demands, and one's own emotions and needs as a learner. Such an assignment will also build into it the support students need to succeed on it while simultaneously nurturing the independence that awaits students on the other side of their struggles.

The Forms and Features of Research Paper Assignments

Though this chapter focuses mostly on major research papers, it is important to note that the long paper comes in different forms and can be designed with a wider range of purposes in mind than the traditional research paper. Some, especially those teaching Advanced Placement courses, assign major papers in which students analyze one or more literary works; others ask students to trace an author's development over time or across multiple works, focusing on the evolution of the author's style or treatment of a theme. When I taught AP English classes, students wrote a major paper about some key idea they found to be especially important in *Crime and Punishment*; my students also wrote longer papers (around five pages) in which, for example, they compared Shakespeare's treatment of a subject in five sonnets they selected from a larger set I provided. Students also wrote a critical analysis of *Heart of Darkness* using a critical lens they chose from a list of options (e.g., feminist theory, postcolonial theory, Marxist theory).

Other forms of the long paper exist, of course, some blending the personal and the academic into new forms or variations on old forms. Some longer papers narrate students' inquiry into a topic of personal interest, such as John Creger's Personal Creed Project, which asks students to reflect on the following:

> a) how they came to be the people they are today, b) what they most value at this point, and c) how they wish to develop themselves in the years ahead. Reflecting systematically over a period of weeks (college versions) or months (high school versions), students identify the people and forces that have been the most important influences in shaping their lives in the past. They identify specific values each of their most significant influences inspire them to stand for in the present. They consider qualities they'd like to develop over the coming decade to help them live by the three to five values they have chosen (their personal creeds). And they envision how they want to make a difference in the world or others' lives in the future. (2014–15, 60–73)

Another powerful inquiry, first developed by K. Wayne Yang and Jeff Duncan-Andrade, is the Doc Ur Block project, which requires students in a high school sociology class to engage in extended research in order to answer the question, "How can sociology be used to examine, challenge and transform the persistence of social, economic, and political inequality?" (Yang and Duncan-Andrade 2006). Tom Romano, also straining against the constraints of the traditional research paper format, developed the multigenre research paper, of which he offers a "formal definition" in his book *Fearless Writing*:

> A multigenre paper arises from research, experience, and imagination. It is not an uninterrupted, expository monologue nor a seamless narrative nor a collection of poems. A multigenre paper is composed of many genres and subgenres, each piece self-contained, making a point of its own, yet connected by

theme or topic and sometimes by language, images, and content. In addition to many genres, a multi-genre paper may also contain many voices, not just the author's. The craft then—the challenge for the writer—is to make such a paper hang together as one unified whole. (2013, 8)

Regardless of the form, these long papers have common features, all of which vary according to the aims of the paper and the context of the assignment. They share certain moves common to academic writing, most of which I touched on in the previous section but merit further consideration here. One fundamental feature of these long academic papers is entering into the larger and longer conversation people have had, and continue to have, about the subject. This means reading and including in the paper others' views and using those as a point of agreement or departure for one's own position. These different moves have been named by Graff and Birkenstein in their book *They Say/I Say: The Moves That Matter in Academic Writing*, a few of which give us a sense of these moves students need to learn to make in the longer paper: "Introducing 'Standard Views,'" "Introducing What 'They Say,'" "Introducing an Ongoing Debate," "Agreeing and Disagreeing Simultaneously," and "Entertaining Objections" (2014).

I provide my seniors with a handout I call Expert Project: Possibilities and Patterns for their Expert Project paper, which offers more detailed support for those who need it when writing such a major paper; struggling writers, especially those with special needs or those still learning English, find it helpful. Those who have taken AP Language and Composition the previous year, along with those who have become proficient academic writers, tend not to need or want to use the guidelines, though they all find aspects of it and *They Say/I Say* helpful when writing such major papers.

Expert Project: Possibilities and Patterns

Perhaps the central feature of the major paper, one that will ask so much of both students and teachers, is the sense of discovery and contribution it should provide students as a result of such in-depth investigation and sustained thought about a topic. The authors of *The Craft of Research* put it this way:

Most of the important things we do, we do with others. Some students think that research is different: they imagine a solitary scholar reading alone in a hushed library or peering into a microscope surrounded only by glassware and computers. But no place is more filled with voices than a library or lab. Even when you work alone, you silently converse with others when you read a book or call up a website. Every time you go to a source for information, you renew a relationship between writers and readers that may be centuries old. And when you report your own research, you can hope that other voices will respond to yours, so that you can in turn respond to them. And so it goes. But conversation is a social activity. Both sides have to understand what each expects of the other, what "social role" each is expected to play. And that's especially true when the conversation is in writing and among professional colleagues. (Booth et al. 2016, 16)

Let's go into my classroom to see what this process looks like as my students experience it through the Expert Project, a yearlong inquiry into one topic that culminates in a major paper.

Classroom Connection: What Research Paper Assignments Look Like in My Class

Here is the overview of the Expert Project as it appears on the first handout I provide my seniors in August:

Our challenge throughout the early years of our life is to find a question or problem that so fascinates us that we would want to spend the rest of our life trying to answer or solve it—or at least play some part in that process. As we learn more about this subject, investigating it over time and from different perspectives, we begin to develop some expertise. The definition and etymology of the word *expert* is worth mentioning:

> **Noun:** a person who has a comprehensive and authoritative knowledge of or skill in a
> particular area (e.g., finance). **Adjective:** having or involving authoritative knowledge: *he*
> *is **expert** at handling the media.*
> **Origin:** Middle English: from French and Latin *expertus*, past participle of *experiri* "**try**."
> The noun use dates from the early nineteenth century. It shares a common root with the
> words *experience* and *experiment*.

The idea for this yearlong investigation derived from my own fumbling apprenticeship into academic literacy after barely graduating from high school and the idea that students need to explore their own interests as part of their journey toward an academic and vocational identity. Kieran Egan puts it this way in his book *Learning in Depth*:

> By learning something in depth we come to grasp it from the inside, as it were, rather than the way
> in which we remain always somehow on the outside of that accumulated breadth of knowledge. With
> regard to the knowledge we learn in breadth, we rely always on the expertise of others; when learning
> in depth, we develop our own expertise. (2010, 6)

The Expert Project, then, is designed as an extended experience, one that is grounded in the academic essentials but also the need to engage and challenge students through personal, meaningful inquiry that either validates what already interests students or creates an opportunity to discover what does interest them. Returning to the different types of long papers discussed in the previous section, I would place the Expert Project somewhere between the traditional research paper in style and structure and the more fluid forms of the Doc Ur Block and multigenre research papers. After ten years, it has become an established rite of passage for all seniors at Burlingame High School, the AP teachers having adapted it to their own courses as a supplement to the focus on literature. An article in the *Burlingame B*, our school paper, offers a useful glimpse of students' perspective on it:

> For Sophia Bonk, the Expert Project had deep personal significance. Her youngest brother has Prader-Willi syndrome, a genetic disease that causes constant hunger, low muscle mass, and other physical and mental disabilities. A little research in AP Biology on possible future solutions to Prader-Willi syndrome led Bonk down the rabbit-hole of what she likes to call "Designer Babies," or embryonic genetic modifications. . . .
>
> Senior Cameron Peña's project is an example of how the process of researching and refining information leads to an evolution in the focus of the study.
>
> "I started getting into how people react to murders, and how people react to actually being the murderer themselves," Peña said, "and that kind of led me into being interested in how people don't feel emotion after they commit a murder."
>
> He explained how psychopathy is formed by the existence of a specific gene that leads to the overproduction of serotonin, a neurotransmitter in the brain that acts as a relaxant at high doses.
>
> "If you're producing excess levels of serotonin, then your brain is in a constant state of relaxation, which should be a nice thing, except when you're constantly relaxed, you're numbed to a lot of events," Peña said.
>
> Contrary to popular belief, it is the overproduction of serotonin coupled with traumatic experiences that leads to psychopathic behaviors. Peña spoke of how a surprising number of CEOs have psychopathic qualities, that is, they must make tough decisions for their companies that might involving laying off many employees. "A big misconception is that psychopaths are purely violent people. And through my research, I've found that, instead of, 'you're a psychopath, you're automatically a killer,' it's more of a spectrum," Peña said. "On one hand, you have your killers, and on the other hand, you have people that exhibit psychopathic traits, but aren't necessarily violent."
>
> While he was conducting research, Peña consulted a professional homicide detective. They talked about some movie portrayals of psychopaths that are relatively authentic; some examples include "Nightcrawler," "No Country for Old Men," and "Psycho."

In keeping with the principles of design thinking, the Expert Project and all its embedded assignments and the accompanying support materials have undergone constant prototyping and testing over the years as spelled out by the Riverdale Country School

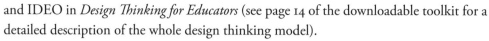

and IDEO in *Design Thinking for Educators* (see page 14 of the downloadable toolkit for a detailed description of the whole design thinking model).

Figure 5–2 is the latest version of the handout we give students as an overview, a road map for the year (and work) ahead.

Throughout much of the fall semester, students focus on finding and refining their subject (see Figure 5–3). Oscar Wilde reportedly quipped that he was "not young enough to know everything," a witty observation that hints at the breadth and depth of knowledge our students think they have when they enter our classroom at the beginning of the year, especially if you teach, as I do, all seniors. Yet the truth is that only about 20 percent of adolescents claim to have an identified, specific interest or sense of purpose, according to the Stanford Center on Adolescence (Flanagan 2017). And most, when first asked to generate ideas for what to spend the year investigating, struggle to come up with a list, perhaps a consequence of the modern attention crisis that technology and modern life have fostered. So we take time to explore different topics, using the Interest Inventory we created and similar resources we have collected and linked to the Expert Project website's resource page over the years.

After about a week, during which students are also doing other work for the course that is unrelated to the Expert Project, students begin writing up their proposal (see Chapter 6 for more on this assignment and a link to the handout). This stage of the process is designed to help them begin to narrow—or, to use design thinking language, define—their focus so that they can begin to investigate their subject through the weekly Critical Notes readings and subsequent independent reading books they will read and write about over the semester. One aim of the fall semester is to take their subject (performance-enhancing drugs, climate change, cyberterrorism, social media, digital currency, emotions, to name just a few of the many subjects) and, by exploring it, refine it and ultimately develop it into a topic (the unintended consequences of performance-enhancing drugs, the blessing and burden of social media) that can be eventually expressed as a guiding question (Why do people cheat? Is social media really good for us?) that they will spend the year trying to answer.

Though all the Critical Notes and independent reading assignments first function as stand-alone writing assignments (see Chapters 1 and 3 respectively for examples and more information on these two assignments), their larger purpose is to prepare students to write the culminating paper in the spring semester. At the point when they are doing this initial investigation work, however, the paper is like some distant country they do not believe they will ever visit, as it seems so impossible and remote to most of them. Thus, the first-semester work is also designed as a sequence that cultivates in students the confidence and identity that this is work they can ultimately do. By the time we get to the

THE EXPERT PROJECT: A YEARLONG INQUIRY INTO ONE SUBJECT

Overview   Our challenge throughout the early years of our life is to find a question or problem that so fascinates us that we would want to spend the rest of our life trying to answer or solve it—or at least play some part in that process. As we learn more about this subject, investigating it over time and from different perspectives, we begin to develop some expertise. The definition and etymology of the word *expert* is worth mentioning:

> **Noun:** a person who has a comprehensive and authoritative knowledge of or skill in a particular area (e.g., finance).
> **Adjective:** having or involving authoritative knowledge: *he is* **expert** *at handling the media*.
>
> **Origin:** Middle English: from French and Latin *expertus*, past participle of *experiri* "**try**." The noun use dates from the early nineteenth century. It shares a common root with the words *experience* and *experiment*.

Requirements   Over the course of the year, you will

- ☐ choose **a topic that fascinates you and satisfies the requirements** of the project (substantive, researchable)
- ☐ submit a **formal proposal** in which you describe and make a case for what you want to study, how, and why
- ☐ explore your topic from different angles through **articles, tweets, blogs, podcasts, books, film,** and **lectures**
- ☐ write and submit **Critical Notes** each week on the stream, video, article, or podcast you examined in depth
- ☐ read **four full-length books** on your topic (two in the fall, two in the spring) and write an in-class essay on each
- ☐ write an **interim report** in which you examine your topic through different lenses
- ☐ conduct field research and analyze it through **surveys, interviews, experiments, or observations**
- ☐ summarize and interpret the meaning and importance of your research in an **executive summary**
- ☐ **present your findings** to the class in preparation for writing your paper
- ☐ submit an **annotated bibliography** of your weekly readings and independent reading (IR) books
- ☐ **produce a final paper** during spring semester that examines your topic through your research and experiences
- ☐ educate people about your topic by **putting your learning into practice** (ad campaign, letter to official, etc.)

Expectations   This project draws on and aims to develop your ability to

- ▶ develop questions about and explore a substantive topic in depth over time
- ▶ understand and analyze the ideas and arguments people have proposed about your topic
- ▶ evaluate the treatment of your topic through different perspectives and media
- ▶ synthesize these different ideas and respond to them with your own evidence or information
- ▶ convey your insights and ideas through words, images, and visual explanations
- ▶ manage your time, obligations, energy, and commitment to quality

Fall Semester   You will gather information about and monitor your topic through the media. As you develop your initial ideas about it, you will begin to discover other aspects of the topic you may wish to explore instead. It is almost inevitable that your topic will evolve as your understanding and exploration of it does. In the fall, each of you will

- ☐ submit a formal proposal that describes your topic, provides a rationale, and lists the four books you will read
- ☐ learn more about your subject by reading, viewing, or listening to one of the following media: article, blog, social media feed, visual or graphic representation (infographic, art, photography, film) produced by an established person in that field for purposes related to your topic
- ☐ submit the weekly Critical Notes on whatever you read, view, hear, watch, or otherwise study
- ☐ read *two books* from your proposal about your topic each grading period; *any* changes must be approved
- ☐ maintain your annotated bibliography for the project, keeping track of and evaluating all your sources
- ☐ write the in-class essays on your two self-selected books
- ☐ write the interim report for the final exam, summing up and discussing what you learned

Topics   Your topic should be worthy of the front page or cover of a newspaper or magazine:

war/military	ethics	health/medicine	information
media	finance/economics	sports	other (you choose and make
transportation	law/crime	religion/faith	the case for investigat-
environment	biography/life study	politics/government	ing this subject)
technology/science	entertainment	intelligence/	

FIGURE 5–2 A unit like the Expert Project paper begins with a handout that maps out the course of the entire process so students know up front what they must do and have a way to keep track of their progress.

first grading period six weeks into the semester, the Expert Project work mostly runs in the background of the class (see Figure 5–4 for a time line of the whole project), surfacing only once a week when they turn in their weekly Critical Notes and engage in small-group discussions about what they read and learned about their subject that week and how it relates to what they had discovered in previous weeks.

As the fall semester unfolds and students continue to investigate their subject through Critical Notes and the two independent reading books they chose (and discussed in their proposal), I meet formally and on the fly with students to discuss their progress with the subject and the project in general. Each week, I provide feedback about some key aspect of the Critical Notes (see Figures 1–15 and 1–16 for an example of this) that merits attention. One week I might give a minilesson on how to read and write critically about a Twitter feed, political cartoon, or TED Talk; another week, I might focus on how to

FIGURE 5–3 Lexi writes about one of the IR books she read and will include in her eventual Expert Project paper about the issues facing adolescent girls. Her personal investment in the topic has made the books and paper much more engaging for her throughout the year.

Time Line of the Expert Project: Overview of the Senior Year

AUGUST	SEPTEMBER	OCTOBER	NOVEMBER	DECEMBER	JANUARY	FEBRUARY	MARCH	APRIL
Introduce Expert Project				Interim Report (RP)				Spring Break
Topic/Proposal (ALT)				Annotated Bibliography (WTL)	Topic Refinement	Primary Research (ALT)		
Critical Notes (7–10 for the Semester) (WTL)						Presentation (ALT)	Expert Project Paper (RP/PP)	
Read IR Book #1	IR #1 Essay (WOD)	Read IR Book #2	IR #2 Essay (WOD)		Read IR Book #3	IR #3 Essay (WOD)		
Uncharted Territory: Education Unit		*Wild Unit/Uncharted* Readings (Freedom)		*Uncharted Territory:* Credo Unit		*Henrietta Lacks* Unit		Power Unit/*1984*

Includes the six different types of academic writing assignments (AWAs) throughout the Expert Project: writing to learn (WTL), writing on demand (WOD), short answer (SA), process paper (PP), research paper (RP), alternate forms (ALT).

FIGURE 5–4 This time line offers some sense of what all these different pieces look like in action and how the demands of the Expert Project run in the background for much of the year, until we begin to focus on the presentation and papers in the spring.

improve their performance on some specific part of the Critical Notes or how to write the upcoming timed writing on their independent reading book as it relates to their subject— or, for some, their emerging topic and guiding question.

When we arrive at December, students have read, written, discussed, and generally thought about their subject a great deal. Some have discarded their initial subject and others radically refined it; a few have merely tweaked theirs a bit, while about a quarter of the students have stayed with what they chose at the beginning and spent the semester drilling down into the topic, such as prosthetics, addiction, shame, comedy—all topics that students have investigated over the years. Yes, we take all this time, stretching it out over the entire semester, so the ideas, the questions, the connections can ferment, compost, and, eventually, reveal themselves. This investment of time has proven invaluable over the years.

Interim Paper
Overview

Annotated
Bibliography
Overview

Now it is time to have students pull over onto the side of the road and examine what they have learned so far, but not in a formal, intimidating way. So, as part of their final, we have them write what we call an "interim report," an informal but substantive narrative of what they read, thought, and learned along the way; however, we also want to achieve a bit more, to bump up the cognitive demands of the paper (which can easily end up being 8–10 pages for many of the kids—longer if you add the annotated bibliography that is also required at this point). The purpose of the interim report and annotated bibliography is to synthesize all they have learned so far in more of a narrative (a variation on what people used to call an I-Search paper) and lay the foundation for the spring semester. When students return after winter break, they begin the more formal process of developing their subject into a topic and a guiding or research question that they will, after further investigating the topic, examine in their culminating paper later in the spring semester.

In the following excerpts from Cameron's interim report into psychopaths, we see Cameron's thinking taking shape along with the moves he needed as a writer to express his thoughts. He started by discussing his initial thoughts, assumptions, expectations, and motivations for investigating the subject of psychopaths:

> My initial thought about criminal psychology was that the field was an incredibly interesting idea, but that it didn't have an application to real life besides its appeal in TV and movies. I thought that the almost magical deductions that these profilers came to was simply a good way for a show like *Criminal Minds* to add some awe. Despite others saying that criminal psychology is just an art and should stay in the TV shows, I disagreed and believed that criminal psychology could become a reliable method in catching criminals. As I grew older, I began to focus myself on the hardest people to analyze, psychopaths.

Psychopathic criminals act in whatever way will help them to achieve their goals, regardless of moral implications. When my interest in psychopaths first began around freshman year, I found that the question that always seemed to be on my mind was—why? I had to grasp why these people performed such heinous acts without being affected by empathy and how they justified themselves.

What Cameron left out of this first part is that he had an uncle who was an FBI agent and who focused on these areas of homicide, a connection that became more important as the project unfolded in the months ahead. After the fall semester, Cameron wrote in his interim report about how his thinking and understanding about the subject of psychopaths had evolved:

While some people may think that criminal psychology is an art and not defined enough to be useful in criminal investigations, I completely disagree. I believe that the only place a truly violent psychopath finds that they cannot hide is their own subconscious. A defining characteristic as outlined by Mark Safarik in his analysis of the serial killer Joel Rifkin is that they are extremely good at conning people. They can't feel emotion, but they have an uncanny ability to respond as if they do because this is necessary to manipulate others. If people were able to analyze based off of subconscious cues that a psychopath couldn't control, they would be as good as caught.

Some find the question of people being able to perfectly analyze a criminal's subconscious actions and interpret them correctly as too unrealistic. It is true that it is almost impossible to use the same psychological techniques on all criminals when they are all unique in the way they act. However, I would point out that what we need are teachers like John Douglas who are experienced enough to not teach techniques to analyze specific situations, but skills to analyze groups and continue from there. These veterans work from their previous experiences so understanding how to analyze different kinds of criminals would be invaluable.

In comparison to other techniques for catching criminals, I recognize that criminal psychology is new. People are skeptical of its practicality because of how little time this field has had to develop its success. But envisioning a future of law enforcement where criminals could be caught based on profiles alone without the long process of obtaining warrants means that criminals will be caught faster.

Looking ahead to the spring semester and the work he'd have to do on the Expert Project, Cameron sketched out the following plan for himself:

As I continue my Expert Project I want to learn more about the drawbacks of increasing the use of criminal profiling in law enforcement. I feel that I looked too much at the side that agreed with my previous hypothesis which only solidified my ideas. I am still faced with the question about how effective criminal profiling really is. So far I have mostly analyzed profiles created after the criminal was caught, but I know little about how they are used for investigations. The part of my topic that interests me the most is the rehabilitation and release of psychopathic criminals. I am curious as to when they are deemed able to go back to society despite them being well known manipulators.

Find Your
Topic Target

Returning from the winter break rested and having done all that foundational work in the fall, students are now ready to take a deeper dive into their subject, turning it into a topic and guiding question. As each of the stages and accompanying handouts shows, this is a carefully designed process, one that we refine each year in light of new insights or such changes as acquiring class sets of computers for all our seniors (see Figure 5–5). When I say "we," I am referring to all the senior teachers, for these are documents and assignments we have collaborated on for many years now, each making suggestions as to what to change or what new steps to add to the project.

By the end of January, students are reading their four (and last) independent reading book, a title that should be listed on their initial proposal; however, by this point, as their topics and questions come into real focus, students often have drifted into new directions and so they need to be free to consider different books, though these must still be approved. My role at this stage of the process is often to serve as a reading mentor and project advisor, guiding them toward the books that will help them extend their inquiry or helping them figure out how to read such nonfiction books in light of their research topic or guiding question. During the individual conferences with students in the early weeks of the spring semester, I make sure they are moving in the right direction, not heading toward a dead end, and often suggest books that will help to lead them in new directions. This role has the added benefit of reinforcing the value of reading and creating opportunities for me to recommend books that I may have just read or seen reviews of, all of which contributes to the culture of literacy I try to foster in my classes.

While students are reading their last independent book, which they will eventually connect to their earlier independent books when they write about it, we are all reading Rebecca Skloot's *The Immortal Life of Henrietta Lacks* (2010). As this book represents the ultimate in research and engaging nonfiction writing about a complex topic, it serves as a model for the type of work they have done with their topic all year. Skloot shows what it looks like to keep unpeeling one's topic to reveal whole new layers; thus, it is the perfect book to read as a model and inspiration for the next stage of the Expert Project: field research.

Field Research
Overview

Now students, having reached the deeper strata of their topics after all this time, are ready to go into the field and do their own original research by conducting interviews,

Name: Lizzie   Period:

Overview

This tool is designed to help you do some initial thinking about your subject as you prepare to begin your project. The idea for right now is to come up with as many ideas as possible, then see which idea interests you the most and seems the most viable topic. The first tool generates ideas; the second one helps you narrow, refine, and begin to develop.

Directions:

1. Write your subject (e.g., food) in the center of the target on top.

2. In first ring ("categories"), put symbols, single words, or very short phrases that identify the smaller slices we can use to consider the topic and generate ideas for the one you finally choose.

3. In the outer ring ("description"), jot down a very brief note that explains something about this category, its importance, and its relevance.

4. Choose one slice from the top organizer and write that in the middle of the tool on the bottom. This should be written as a phrase (e.g. "the effect of technology on relationships").

5. In the four "Aspect" boxes, generate four aspects or sides of the topic, then fill each box in with ideas, questions, or examples.

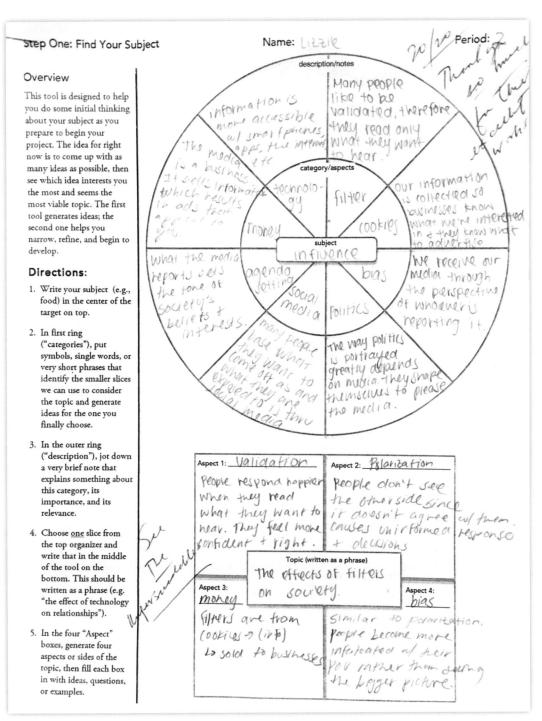

FIGURE 5–5 Lizzie's example shows her first expanding and exploring her subject and then narrowing and refining it below into a topic that grew into an excellent paper about the influence of the media.

surveys, experiments, or observations. This part of the Expert Project is designed to create opportunities for me to teach students, through applications such as Google Forms or SurveyMonkey, how to design surveys and write questions for interviews that will yield useful information or data they will summarize, analyze, and explain the meaning and importance of in the subsequent report and interpretation.

Expert Project
Presentation
Overview

Now that they have read all their books and done all their research, and reflected on and analyzed the meaning and importance of their topic and findings all these many months, we turn toward the final stretch. Instead of having students write the paper, though, we require them to deliver a detailed multimedia presentation to a small group of their peers. During these presentations, those not presenting are taking structured notes and then giving the speakers feedback on their ideas, posing questions about their topic or their approach to it (see Figures 5–6 and 5–7).

Why a presentation at this point? With spring break roughly a month away, students are getting antsy, especially since they are seniors. We are now into March, with the heavy lifting of the paper just around the corner. By asking them to synthesize all they have learned into an engaging and serious presentation to a small group, we give them a chance to rehearse the paper they are about to write in the coming weeks. In other words, they are orally drafting the general moves of the paper they will write. As a result, they come to the writing process of the major paper having already drafted its moves and main ideas in their presentation, with the slides functioning as a sort of mixed-media outline for the paper. Within the context of the presentation, they also learn how to design slides and write as one must on a slide for a real audience of one's peers. The days of presentations also have a tremendous effect of building a shared sense of accomplishment for having arrived at a point where they realize how much they have to say and how much they have learned along the way.

After the students finish their presentations, they gather all their notes and other information and begin the process of writing the final paper they have spent all year preparing and learning how to write. In the last ten years, out of roughly one hundred seniors each year, I would guess we have had maybe five students not write this paper. The actual assignment for the paper, which we take three weeks to write, turns the class into a workshop where the only focus is the writing of the paper. Over those three weeks, students are writing, conferring with me, learning about specific aspects of the paper through minilessons, filling in the gaps on their research as needed, and revising through guided processes and strategies I teach them as I monitor and give feedback on their progress along the way. Throughout this process of composition, they are guided by the Expert Project Paper Checklist we provide them, since at this point they need structure to make sure they get everything done as specified.

Expert Project
Paper
Checklist

FIGURE 5–6 John presents his work on nonverbal communication to his group. Some share their slides with the group for all to look at; others prefer to present from their screen, as John is doing here.

FIGURE 5–7 While Tyler presents, Eric and Joshua take notes to give her as feedback and ideas to use when writing her paper.

Over the years, I have developed small but important rituals around the completion of the Expert Project to reinforce the sense of it as a rite of passage and the culmination of a year's journey. First, I ask them to show their final draft to their parents or some other adult that might take time to read and respond to it before they hand it in. I want them to get that recognition for having not just written such a paper but taken that step toward the deeper, more mature learning adulthood demands. I want them to know the feeling of being taken seriously. Some parents just sign the first page; others, however, write proud notes to their son or daughter, sometimes writing to me, as well, to thank me for challenging their child at this crucial juncture.

Before I collect the papers, I ask students to reflect on their performance, process, and progress as writers, readers, thinkers, and students. Then, as they finish, students come up one at a time to present their paper, which I mark off to show I received it, taking time to make sure they completed all the requirements and submitted the finished paper to Turnitin, where I will give all my feedback by audio within the application. But we also briefly sit and have a conversation, even if only for a minute, about the experience. As a rule, I do not allow students to revise their final Expert Project paper, in part because they have written it in a very recursive way, revising as they went in response to various forms and sources of feedback. Occasionally, however, a student will have some type of problem or pattern of error in his or her paper that offers the perfect opportunity to learn his or her way up to the next level of performance; in such an instance, I am willing to tell the student, often an English learner, that if he or she is willing to meet with me and revise the paper, I will reevaluate it. Students always accept the invitation.

What do students say about the paper and the Expert Project as a whole? Paige, who spent the year researching the treatment of animals in captivity, a topic about which she cared deeply, wrote:

> Looking over this process, I am very proud of the paper I am turning in today—April 11th. I feel I have presented an intriguing, persuasive argument with passion that demonstrates my strong connection to my topic. I am very happy with the topic I chose. Although my opinion did not change, my perspectives were challenged and broadened, allowing me to learn many new things. I know this topic will continue to be a big part of my life, even after I submit this paper, because it is an issue I care deeply about.

Lucas, a student with whom I had many great conversations about his topic (the factors that shape our character and our lives) and the books he read throughout the year (*Hillbilly Elegy*, *NutureShock*, and *Between the World and Me*), entered my class after three years of honors and AP English classes. It means a great deal to find all students challenged and satisfied in the ways Lucas described:

> *Based on your work on the Expert Project in general and your paper in particular, how ready do you feel for the demands of college-level work?*
>
> Very prepared. I am very excited for college and I feel like my Expert Project (the repercussions of environment) will greatly influence me in college and deciding where I'm going to go. I am very satisfied with what I found and how I am going to apply it to my life.
>
> *Should we continue to assign the Expert Project to all CP seniors?*
>
> Yes, the Expert Project should be assigned to all seniors. There is a type of freedom and ability for seniors to explore their own thoughts and ideas that is similar to college. I really like that we were able

to explore our own interests and dive deeper into our own questions about life. Great project, I highly recommend continuing it throughout the years.

The focus here has been somewhat different than the other chapters, for it is the experience, the sustained inquiry into and writing of a major paper about a complex topic that is the more important aspect of the design for the long paper. Yet the Expert Project as well as those writing assignments embedded throughout it satisfy the guidelines I have spelled out throughout these chapters when it comes to designing effective academic writing assignments. As an Academic Writing Assignment, the Expert Project is

- *anchored in clear goals linked to specific standards* appropriate to students' age and development, as well as the future exams they will take in class, for the state, or on national assessments;
- *grounded in texts* that are as engaging as they are demanding in terms of how those texts must be read and used in the writing task;
- *cognitively demanding* relative to the standards themselves and students' intellectual progress without being overwhelming and thus leaving students feeling defeated;
- *emotionally and intellectually engaging to all students* to the degree that the assignments give students some measure of choice when it comes to the texts, tasks, and topics they encounter in the context of the writing assignment;
- *designed to support students* in ways that help them meet the challenges of the writing task while also demonstrating their knowledge and skills legitimately and independently despite such potential obstacles as language or learning difficulties;
- *assessed or evaluated according to criteria and requirements that are clearly stated* up front so students can use them as a guide and know how best to spend their time and energy when writing the assignment; and
- *written and formatted for maximum readability and ease of use* in language that is clear, consistent, concise, and correct, using a layout that makes clear what students need to do and how they need to do it.

Obstacles and Opportunities

The obstacles are all those that one would imagine for the long paper. The nature and scale of the demands are daunting for some, overwhelming for others, and simply ridiculous to a few at one point or another. The different steps and stages of the Expert Project paper and its supplemental assignments throughout require skills and knowledge that most do not have. Many lack the stamina and attention in the early stages to do such in-depth and sustained work. And teachers, of course, are always pressed for time, burdened by the demands of assigning and responding to even the short assignments we give; how then, are we to find time to require such major papers as I have discussed here?

And yet we must find a way, for it is in these assignments that the greatest opportunities for transformation lie. After ten years, after several thousand seniors have passed through our senior classes at my school, what we hear is gratitude for the opportunity to explore not only a topic but the world outside of school as well as the one within themselves. There is no better example of such exploration than Nina's inquiry into the topic of love, something she felt she did not understand but needed to learn more about as she prepared to leave her family for the larger and as yet unknown world that awaited her at college the following year:

> My initial idea at the beginning of the year was very focused on expressing love, but over time, it developed into the problems of love, so bringing as much as I could from my notes and sources was hard. However, I really do enjoy this topic and it raised my awareness of love and relationships and how much more difficult they are now. I have learned a lot about how love has changed in the fast-paced world today and why it seems to be doing so poorly. I think it has also made me realize how old fashioned I am. My friends seem to be more into the fast-paced love of today, but I seem to prefer the slow love of the past. I've also confirmed how fickle love can be and have realized that part of the reason we have so many problems with love is because of the generation we were raised in and the rapidly growing world around us.

As an outcome to the year's work, Nina's response was one I was glad to accept as a measure of success: she learned about love, a topic of great personal interest to her, and in the process learned, if not to love writing, at least to do it much better.

Reflect on Your Own Practice

Take some time to consider the types of writing assignments I have discussed in this chapter and how they compare with the assignments from your own class when it comes to the longer forms of writing. Specifically, I suggest that you do the following steps in your head, in writing, or as part of a discussion with members of your department or those instructional teams (sometimes called PLCs) to which you belong.

1. Generate a list of the research-based or long-form writing assignments you have students do in a semester or during a specific unit you just finished or are about to begin. You might take a minute to examine the assumptions behind these different assignments or the degree to which they complement other, larger assignments in your overall curriculum. Make notes as needed about ways you could improve your use or the design of such assignments based on your observations.

2. Examine the assignments on the list you created or a smaller subset of representative assignments in light of the AWA Framework checklist to assess the degree to which these writing assignments include or could be improved to better incorporate the features listed on the AWA Framework.

6 Alternative Forms of Academic Writing

Implementing New Forms, Features, and Functions

> *If we want our students to understand the value that writing can play in their lives, maybe we should consider shifting instruction away from strict adherence to traditional discourses and begin having our students explore the reasons real writers write. When students understand the real-world purposes for writing (instead of simply writing to meet the next school requirement) they begin to internalize the relevance of writing, and more important, they develop an understanding that writing is an important skill to carry into adulthood. When students begin to understand this relevance, their writing improves.*
>
> —KELLY GALLAGHER, *Teaching Adolescent Writers*

Alternative Assignments: What They Are and Why We Assign Them

All the previous chapters examine the assignments we design for our students most of the time. As any book about genres must acknowledge, however, outliers abound and hybrids arise, for teachers are a creative bunch, looking everywhere for ideas for a lesson, an assignment, a paper. I've been out to restaurants with teachers and heard someone at the table say, while deciding what to order, "This menu is *really* interesting—the way every dish is described, the way it's laid out. It's giving me some ideas about how I might adapt this for my next unit!" And a murmur of appreciation and recognition then fluttered around the table as others saw the same potential. Another at the same table chimed in, "You know, I saw this crazy infographic the other day in a magazine and it got me thinking about trying something like that with this unit I'm teaching now." Once, while waiting in a Starbucks for my coffee, I started looking at a pamphlet they had on their different coffees and their origins, complete with narratives, graphics, images, and tables.

"I gotta do something like *this*," I thought to myself by the time they called me up to the counter for my latte!

Yes, we teachers are always on the lookout for ideas, forms, features, and functions we can add to our assignments or from which we might design whole new assignments we had not considered possible until we saw an example. These divergent creations, such as a mixed-media paper using Google Slides, Google Keep, Visme, Prezi, or Piktochart, are all viable alternatives to the forms discussed here so long as they adhere to the basic moves of academic writing and rhetoric.

In recent years, my own inclination is to look for opportunities that reflect the demands of the world for which we are preparing our students in the assignments I design. The more I look, the more connections I find through my experiences as a consumer and a citizen; moreover, in discussions with people in different fields, I encounter even more ideas. These discoveries take what initially seem to be nonacademic forms, such as proposals, letters, memos, executive summaries, multimedia slide sets, podcasts, blogs, and infographics. Yet one quickly sees within these forms their potential to accommodate academic moves, thinking moves, the moves students need to make as writers who, in an increasingly fluid communication landscape, must be able to use an ever-increasing array of tools to communicate their ideas and arguments.

In this chapter, then, I want to expand our notions of what is appropriate for academic writing assignments, offering a range of possibilities, though some may be familiar to you. What is the rationale for these alternative forms? In short, connections to the real world of work, citizenship, and consumer needs. Ideas here come from my experiences with writing proposals for books and grants, letters to companies and to local parking agencies to contest tickets, surveys and summaries of data from those surveys for school or books. Other, more familiar and traditional forms have their place here, too: résumés, letters of introduction, outlines, and slide sets for presentations. But I have tweaked most of these to more effectively accommodate the moves of academic writing and thinking, as you will see.

Recently, I needed a résumé to submit for a new position in our district for working with struggling high school students in a program located on the local community college campus; however, I had not needed a résumé since I originally applied for my teaching position twenty-five years ago! Surveying the résumé scene for formats and features typical of today's résumés, I realized much had changed when it came to writing—and designing—such a document. Figure 6–1 is what I came up with after several days of research and revision, one based on readability on paper or screen, based on the assumption that it would get not much more than a minute of attention, and based on the notion that I needed to address certain assumptions about my qualifications to work with such a program. (As it

JIM BURKE

(415) 555-1111   jim_burke@smuhsd.org   www.englishcompanion.com

PROFILE

After graduating near the bottom of my high school, I discovered learning and education. I have devoted my life to teaching, writing, and mentoring teens, especially seniors, ever since.

PURPOSE

I am committed to preparing students, especially seniors, to learn the skills they need to make a living and make a life for themselves, their families, and the communities they serve.

PASSIONS

Document design. Poetry. **Story**. The Lyric Essay. *Language*. **Reading**. *Writing*. **Teaching**. Family. Cycling. **Design thinking**. **Kids**. **Education**. *Conversation*. **Fly fishing**. Theater.

EXPERIENCE

Teacher

I have taught English–AP and CP, grades 9–12–at Burlingame High School for 24 years, primarily AP Literature and CP Senior English in the last ten, CP English exclusively for the last five years. I created the ACCESS Program (Academic Success) at BHS, which was similar to AVID. For many years, I cotaught an integrated English–social studies class at BHS with social studies teacher Frank Firpo. I have also taught special education (at a private school and in the Peace Corps). I have designed and taught online courses for teachers and in collaboration with the US Holocaust Memorial Museum in Washington, DC, as part of my work with the English Companion Ning.

Author • Speaker • Consultant

Over the last 20 years, I have written and published over 25 books, nearly all of which focus on teaching the essential academic literacies of reading, writing, speaking, thinking, and learning. In addition to writing, I speak at conferences and work with districts and schools around the United States as a consultant to help improve literacy instruction. My most recent books include *Uncharted Territory: A High School Reader* (2017) and the high school edition of *They Say/I Say: The Moves That Matter in Academic Writing* (2014), which I worked on with Graff and Birkenstein. Both are published by W. W. Norton.

Facilitator • Organizer • Creator

I have created multiple professional networks for English teachers and the English profession at large through Twitter, Tumblr, Facebook, and the Ning platform. The English Companion Ning, with nearly 50,000 members, is the largest online community of English teachers in existence. The skills I developed when creating the EC Ning have helped me better understand the complexities of creating and maintaining a thriving professional community.

Mentor • Guide • Advisor

I have played these roles for individuals as well as the school at large through my work on the Site Council, with the Latino Parents Group, the Parent Ed Group, and student teachers. My work in this role is especially important to me in relation to my seniors, with whom I meet and communicate regularly during conferences, via email, or in conversations around school.

HIGHLIGHTS

Advisor WRITE Center for Secondary Students

Advisory Board NextLesson & SchoolLoop

AP English Course & Exam Review Commission

Author of 25 Books

Best Social Network Awards

California Reading Teacher Hall of Fame Award

CATE Lifetime Achievement Award

Chief Advisor College Board ELA PreAP Program

Creator English Companion Ning Social Network

National Board Professional Teaching Standards

NCTE Exemplary Leader Award

NCTE Intellectual Freedom Award

EDUCATION

Master of Arts
Secondary Education
San Francisco State University

Graduate Certificate
Teaching of Written Composition
San Francisco State University

ERWC Certificate
CSU ERWC Training Program
San Mateo County Office of Education

Single Subject Credential
English and Psychology
San Francisco State University

Bachelor of Arts
Cognitive Psychology
University of Santa Barbara

1 Main Street   San Francisco, CA   94105

FIGURE 6–1 Jim Burke's résumé as sample

happened, they ended up canceling the interviews and, soon after, the program because of lack of funding, so my résumé went unread by anyone except my wife.)

What Students Say and How They Struggle with Alternative Assignments

Many of these assignments appeal to the more practical, linear minds among my students, for the emphasis is often on effective communication skills for real purposes and, when possible, to real audiences. These students praise the real-world application and respect the future value of such assignments, saying when I seek feedback how much they appreciated learning something they would actually be able to *use* someday. Of course, I think they can use all that they learn in our classes, but kids are a little more skeptical when we exclaim how helpful something will be years from now!

Those students who are, perhaps, more advanced or inclined toward the creative side of things sometimes resist these alternative assignments, dismissing them as too focused on skills, as if the work were almost appropriate for a remedial class or some study skills course they had been sentenced to take. Oftentimes, if these students have been in AP Language prior to entering my senior English class, they have a moment when they think something along the lines of, "I *knew* I should have stayed in that AP Lit class! This is ridiculous. . . ." In the passage from his last entry of the year in his Digital Daybook, Aidan, a senior who was initially intent on getting out of my class, wrote this:

> Day to day you were able to teach some of the most valuable lessons I have ever learned, through stories, creative demonstrations, media you have found and other texts and templates you used. Not only were there lessons, but you let us explore our intellect, challenge conventions, and encouraged us to think bigger, deeper and harder about incredibly meaningful topics. You always found a way to incorporate writing and reading into all of the things you did that completely enhanced my personal abilities in the English subjects. So not only was I becoming a completely better English student, but I was intrigued and entertained while doing it. This class was probably very hard and boring if you didn't care, but for me, with a drive to learn, I found A110 to be my academic utopia. I will always remember you for challenging me, enhancing my perspectives on the real world, and making me a genuine, conscious and even more driven academic and social citizen.

We get so many different types of students in each class. It can be difficult to know how to reach and teach them all. What Aidan's letter reminds me is that I need to teach the practical, real-world stuff (he was planning to study business and computer science) but also to incorporate that into the course in ways that surprise and challenge students at all levels.

The Forms and Features of Alternative Assignments

Duarte
Slidedoc
Overview and
Templates

What alternative writing assignments have in common, in many cases, is their use of technology and their adherence to traditional forms (e.g., the résumé, the presentation slide, the survey) but with tweaks that are likely to make these old forms new and more accessible and interesting to students. One of my favorite alternative formats is called a Slidedoc where you can download free templates and guidelines. Examples of such alternative assignments include the following:

▶ *surveys* using Google Forms, SurveyMonkey, or other such applications

▶ *presentations* using PowerPoint, Google Slides, Keynote, Prezi, or Piktochart

▶ *executive summaries or reports* that use words, infographics, and quantitative data from the surveys, questionnaires, or other instruments used for research

▶ *letters* of introduction, complaint, challenge, or thanks to recent guest speakers

▶ *proposals* for topics, courses of action, selected sets of titles, or research projects

Yet even within these forms, one finds still more potential for tweaking them to allow more possibilities. Instead of traditional slide presentations, one can assign students Ignite presentations; according to the Ignite site (www.ignitetalks.io), "Presenters get 20 slides, which automatically advance every 15 seconds. The result is a fast and fun presentation which lasts just 5 minutes." Or you can extend this idea to the PechaKucha format, a twenty-by-twenty design that PechaKucha (www.pechakucha.org) describes as "a simple presentation format where you show 20 images, each for 20 seconds. The images advance automatically and you talk along to the images." These formats can have the feeling of an intellectual poetry slam and the Web is filled with examples students can study and templates they can adopt or adapt.

While letters to officials and others are valid and important opportunities, Kate Hoffman Walker adds an interesting and challenging spin in her classes: She has students write college personal statement essays and application letters to prompts they choose—*as the literary characters they are studying*, making sure to anchor their writing in the texts they are studying. In response, the students then take on the persona of the admissions officer, explaining with supporting details why they did or did not find, for example, Holden

Caulfield or Hamlet a suitable applicant to their university. An alternative to this assignment, which I have used in my class, asks students to write a letter in the voice and from the perspective of a literary character they choose. For example, when my students read Hermann Hesse's *Siddhartha*, they wrote letters home to his parents as if they were Siddhartha, discussing what he had learned and how he had changed from his experiences over the course of the novel, their observations and insights anchored in the text as they wrote. Once, as an alternative to this assignment, I gave students the opportunity to complete an online personality survey as a character they chose from a book—we were reading *Antigone* at the time—and then write up a report in a persona and voice appropriate for a psychologist, offering an initial assessment of the character with details from the story to corroborate their conclusions. Here's a small part of Rachel's psychological evaluation of Antigone to give you a sense of what a student would write for such an assignment:

PSYCHOLOGICAL EVALUATION: CONFIDENTIAL

Date: November 5   **Age:** 21

Client: Antigone   **Marital Status:** Engaged

DOB: Unknown   **Place of Examination:** Peninsula Hospital

Gender: Female

Presenting Problem

21-year-old Antigone is a Greek, Caucasian female struggling with decision-making and attachment issues due to the recent death of her brother Polynices and the death of her father some years before. She has gone back and forth, finally deciding that the correct decision was to bury her brother according to the sacred customs, despite the king's order against it. Creon, king of Thebes (her hometown), has denied her wishes; therefore, she is in a very agitated state and shows signs of possible depression. She is a very intelligent young woman who is very strong-willed when it comes to achieving her goals. She is very straightforward and shows no hesitation when it comes to speaking her mind. She described herself in our initial interview as "goal-oriented" and "won't stop till it's completed."

Other digital forms, some old (blogs) and others new (HyperDocs, http://hyperdocs .co), present rich opportunities for academic writing that also incorporates mixed media, links, and other features. Now that everyone has cameras (still and video) in their pockets, photo-essays and documentary films are more possible, introducing more media-based alternatives to the written versions of such forms. A quick search of the Web using "photo-essays" yields abundant examples from established sources such as *Time* to the more hip and business-oriented *Fast Company* website. A more advanced, data-driven but no less academic variation of these forms is the infographic, many of which now accomplish in one diagram what we used to need a paragraph, a page, or even a whole paper to explain. The gold mine for examples appears each year in the annual *Best Infographics of [Year]* collection, published on paper or searchable online through sites such as Visme.

One last form merits attention: podcasts. Though this is not a form I have incorporated into my class, it allows students to make many of the same moves they would on the page with their voice on a recorder or their phone. As podcasts like Malcolm Gladwell's *Revisionist History* demonstrate, these are not rambles and rants about a topic; rather, they are well-crafted spoken essays that explore a topic as one would in writing a paper, but in this case they can include sounds, interviews, and excerpts of songs and films. One example of a related alternative assignment was the option I provided for Mikka, a young woman in my class who had suffered a traumatic brain injury (TBI), to produce an audio essay in lieu of the ten-page paper for the Expert Project. Mikka's TBI had impaired her writing abilities but not her analytical and observational abilities—or her love of head-banging, heavy-metal rock. While everyone else worked on their Expert Project papers, Mikka produced an audio essay using her phone and some fancy software she knew how to use. Instead of letting me listen to it alone at home, she played it for me during lunch (it took the whole thirty-minute lunch period) one day. When it was over, we enjoyed a thoughtful and lively conversation about the content and the experience of producing what many would probably compare to an extended NPR story about her subject.

That night, after listening to Mikka's essay again, I wrote her a letter of which I will quote just a part here, as it relates to the validity of such alternative assignments:

Dear Mikka,

What I so appreciate about your audio essay about the "Power of Music" is your commitment to doing something different, to trying something new, but also to bringing the same intellectual rigor and ambition to the project that I would expect from you if you were writing it as the ten-page essay required of everyone. I was immediately drawn in by your recorded voice confessing, in the opening minute, that "this was a very difficult experience, that it was incredibly awkward and was definitely a struggle . . . that you were going to stutter to find the right words."

The fact that I get to "hear your essay," spoken in your own pleasant voice, is a unique pleasure; for we often speak of a writer's "voice," but do not mean the *actual* voice when we say this. For another student, whose learning difficulties made the prospect of a ten-page paper overwhelming, I did something *sort of* like yours: he created video about the history of the guitar and its different styles of music, discussing and illustrating and playing as he went. Though it was successful in different ways, it was not as engaging as yours; it makes me realize that visuals, if done to inform but not to *engage*, are not necessarily more interesting than just audio.

I found it particularly interesting to listen to the "moves" you made as a writer speaking your thoughts aloud. My recollection of our agreement/plan was that you should be allowed to orally compose your essay as a sort of work-around for or way to bypass your TBI, which makes writing so difficult at times for you. I can imagine how overwhelming it must feel to try to write a ten-page paper under such circumstances.

What alternatives such as this and the video essay I mention in the letter to Mikka remind us is that we can expect students to do remarkable work if we create the conditions they need and allow them to use the forms that work best within the constraints they face.

Classroom Connection: What Alternative Assignments Look Like in My Class

In my experience, these alternative forms sometimes stem from the necessity-is-the-mother-of-all-invention situations. For example, I ran out of time for students to write the essay I had planned to have them write at the end of *The Immortal Life of Henrietta Lacks* but wanted them to do that same sort of essay thinking, to work on making those same moves—so I came up with the Annotated Skeletal Essay.

The Annotated Skeletal Essay

See Figure 6–2a for the handout I provided students for the Annotated Skeletal Essay assignment.

This solution has proven very useful, giving me a way to modulate my workflow at a crucial time, while still requiring students to do some serious thinking within the realm of academic writing, all of it grounded in a complex text like *The Immortal Life of Henrietta Lacks* and aligned with a few key standards. While it seems easy, students find the assignment more demanding than they expect. By providing students with a useful example, I helped set the standard, which led to results such as this from Rachel (note the first two paragraphs of her complete assignment in Figure 6–2b).

Surveys and Executive Summaries of the Data and Their Importance

As I discuss in the chapter about research papers and other long-form writing, students must gather data by at least one of the following means: survey, questionnaire, observations, or experiments. In our fast-paced world, people increasingly write important documents in

The Immortal Life of Henrietta Lacks: The Annotated Skeletal Essay

Overview	Throughout your reading of *Henrietta Lacks*, you were required to keep both Rhetorical Notes and Story Line Notes as a way of thinking about and interacting with the book as you read it. These response techniques were intended to help you enter into a conversation with the book, its author, and the questions both raised—but without intruding too much on your reading and enjoyment of the book. Using those notes, the book, and your in-class writing for Parts 1 and 2, you will now do something I am calling the Annotated Skeletal Essay. The idea is somewhat simple: You will create the sort of outline described and illustrated below and annotate it in a two-column format to focus more on the moves you need to make as a writer and a thinker on this paper and the Expert Project paper we will begin writing next week. In other words, I want you to think more deeply and precisely about a smaller set of writing moves to help you improve your ability to construct and develop an argument so you can focus on the quality of your thinking more than the quality of your writing.
Requirements	This paper should ☐ be 6–8 paragraphs (in the annotated outline form described below) ☐ be typed, double-spaced, with 12-point font that is appropriate for an academic paper ☐ include your name and page numbers in the header ☐ be formatted as two table columns, with the outline in the left and the annotations on the right; these should line up so that the annotations in the right column clearly align with and comment on the appropriate section of the outline in the left column <table><tr><td>Skeletal Essay</td><td>Annotations/Commentary</td></tr><tr><td></td><td></td></tr></table> ☐ cite all direct quotations using the MLA parenthetical format; if you cite any other sources besides *The Immortal Life of Henrietta Lacks*, please include the full citation
Standards	This assignment focuses on developing your ability to learn or improve your performance in the following standards: ▶ Write arguments to support claims in an analysis of substantive topics or texts, using valid reasoning and relevant sufficient evidence from reliable sources. ▶ Produce clear and coherent writing in which the development, organization, and style are appropriate to task, purpose, and audience.

Guidelines	This assignment asks you to do the following:
	
	☐ Choose one of the items listed on the left of the Story Line Notes (presumably the topic you already wrote about for Parts 1 and 2).
	☐ Create a skeletal essay (think of it as a loose outline) about that topic on the left that includes
	
	    ☐ your subject broken into two parts: a word and a phrase
	
	        ▶ **Example:** Knowledge (word) / The ownership of knowledge (phrase)
	
	    ☐ a claim about this subject that you can support with evidence from the text and shows insight about *The Immortal Life of Henrietta Lacks*
	    ☐ direct and indirect quotations and examples from the text with appropriate page numbers cited correctly
	    ☐ an introduction, body paragraphs, and conclusion (see following example)
	
	☐ Annotate each section of your skeletal essay in the corresponding section on the right. On the right side, your annotations or commentary would do one or more of the following:
	
	    ☐ explain what you are trying to accomplish or say, how and why you are doing/saying that, and what it means or why it matters (see the sample below)
	    ☐ reflect or comment on why you think the general idea(s) in your skeletal essay on the left are so interesting or important

FIGURE 6–2a Annotated Skeletal Essay handout

Word	Knowledge
Phrase	The pursuit of knowledge
Working Argument	Knowledge is a double-edged sword. When we find what we are looking for, there is always a cost.

Skeletal Essay	Annotations/Commentary
Paragraph 1: Introduction What is knowledge? Is there a difference between knowledge and information? Are the gains of knowledge worth the costs? Is curiosity, as a criterion for pursuing knowledge, something to be taken lightly? Should there be limits on the pursuit of knowledge? If so, what should they be? Does the way in which the pursuit of knowledge was carried out affect how we view the results we get from it? How can we dismiss the malpractices of others if nothing is done to ensure they won't happen again? How do the costs of knowledge affect different groups?	These are the questions that I want to explore briefly in my introduction paragraph and in my essay as a whole. I believe that these questions will start me down a path to determine the benefits and the costs of knowledge and if the costs ever outweigh the benefits. These questions are important for historical as well as modern ethical dilemmas and are a perfect lens through which to view *The Immortal Life of Henrietta Lacks*.

Paragraph 2: Cost to Researcher
 	
Focus line: Scientists and researchers rarely pay a physical cost for knowledge, nevertheless, they pay one that can have horrific results: the loss of empathy.
 	
The Nuremberg Trials
 	
  ○ In 1947, seven Nazi doctors were hung for "conducting unthinkable research on Jews without consent" (Skloot 131)
 	
    Many American doctors ignored the resulting Nuremberg Code, as it was not law
 	
  ○ Those who knew about the code believed it only "applied to barbarians and dictators, not to American doctors" (Skloot 131)
 	
    Excuse for doctors to do as they pleased without patient consent
 	
Syphilis experiments
 	
  ○ Skloot tells Pattillo about how "[researchers] recruited hundreds of African-American men with syphilis, then watched them die slow, painful, and preventable deaths, even after they realized penicillin could cure them" (Skloot 50)
 	
    The lack of empathy was fueled by the power the researchers felt
	In this paragraph, I am trying to examine how the loss of empathy by both doctors and researchers leads to suffering on behalf of the subjects, who are considered by the researchers to be deplorable and dispensable. I also wanted to explain the sense of moral superiority that American doctors felt, despite being by no means innocent.
	
	I like where this paragraph is going, but it could be improved if I could find an example of a doctor or researcher's point of view, remorseful or otherwise. It might also be interesting to do a greater comparison between the Nazi doctors and those in America at the same time.

FIGURE 6–2b Rachel's Annotated Skeletal Essay handout

such short forms for real purposes. In his book *Microstyle: The Art of Writing Little*, Christopher Johnson describes such writing as "messages of just a word, a phrase, or a short sentence or two—*micromessages*—[that] lean heavily on every word and live or die by the tiniest stylistic choices" (2011, 1). One of the most real-world assignments students do in my class comes in two parts: creating and using a data-collecting instrument (survey or questionnaire) and then analyzing and writing about the data.

After they have researched what other sources have to say, primarily through books, online sources, and other readings, students are ready to formulate their own questions to generate the data for those questions they have yet to answer or that have begun to arise after all that research. For this writing assignment, they are writing very short forms, mostly questions or other such survey formats designed to yield respondents' views; however, once they have the data, they use them to write longer forms with specific rhetorical aims on the report. We treat the creation of the survey questions in the context of a workshop, for it is essential to get the wording just so if the instrument is to be valid. I distribute the handout for the process of creating their survey or questionnaire on paper so they can keep it handy and refer to it as they go along, checking off each step along the way.

Field Research
Overview

Again, it is important to remember that we are designing an experience, in this instance, one that asks students to occupy the persona of a field researcher who must not only create the instrument but distribute or use it with real people (students often get hundreds of responses after distributing the links and invitations to complete their surveys through their social media streams).

Primary
Research
Summary:
Report and
Interpretation
of Findings

After gathering all their data, which come nicely arranged in spreadsheets when they use a program like Google Forms or SurveyMonkey, students are then ready to summarize and interpret their findings in an executive summary or brief report. This provides a perfect opportunity to adapt real-world forms and formats to this classroom assignment. To this end, I found a model that combined document design, rhetorical aims, interpretation, and analysis all framed in a report such as many have to write at work.

What transformed this assignment from a traditional paper into something new and relevant to the real world of writing was the discovery of a model I could use. I searched around for samples, mostly typing "executive summary design" or similar terms into the search engine, trying to find document designs appropriate to students' data. As it happened, I came across a report on the First Amendment while preparing for my *1984* unit and quickly realized the design offered a strong model for this portion of the Expert Project. It required students to write certain ways for specific purposes—summarize the key findings, interpret the meaning, and discuss the importance of the data—while also emphasizing document design for the way we need to communicate in the modern world as well as the integration of words, images, and data.

When designing such assignments, I always need to test them out to see if my idea will work. This has the added benefit of giving me a sample to provide students that is specific to their task and thus shows them what to do, what a finished sample looks like, and how it should be written. Having created such a sample, I then uploaded it as a template into Google Docs so that students could focus on how to write this assignment without having to get bogged down in the actual design; however, students were free to adapt the template for their own purposes and create their own, so long as it conformed to the same assignment requirements. As a result of providing such a template and guidance, I could reasonably expect students to turn in work that looked like Annabelle's, shown in Figure 6–3.

Proposals

I want to end this section by discussing the design of one last type of real-world writing or alternative writing assignment: proposals. Both in business and in people's personal lives, they must propose ideas, courses of action, projects, and more to people who will, based on how well these proposals are written and reasoned, render a decision as to whether, for example, the author of the proposal will receive funding for the proposed project or be accepted into a program. Central to the proposal are the moves we find in most academic argument assignments, the primary difference being that the proposals we write in the real world—in my case, to propose a book idea, get a class set of Chromebooks, to get funding for new books, to present at a national convention—go to real audiences. When my students reach those moments in their own lives, whether during or after high school, I want them to be ready.

To that end, I designed the project proposal assignment for my seniors as part of their Expert Project process. It has the effect of forcing them to think through and spell out, both for themselves and me, what they want to do, why, and how they will get it done. As the example that follows shows, the handout is designed to both inform them about and illustrate what they must accomplish. In other words, it includes the directions and details of what they must do; however, these are formatted and displayed along the left margin for reference. These details in the margin serve to annotate and explain the model I provide in the body of the document. Thus, students see what I expect, what it looks like, and how it should be written. Figure 6–4 is the handout I provide for them to use when writing their proposals.

PSYCHOPATHY

Primary Research Paper

Prepared by: Annabelle

EXECUTIVE SUMMARY

The 2017 "Psychopathy" survey was conducted by Annabelle McAlindon of Burlingame High School. Those polled were 20 high school seniors. This survey was meant to understand their attitudes and views of psychopathy and psychopaths, and observe the knowledge they had about the topic at hand. Among the key findings were:

- Only 75% of high school seniors knew what the definition of psychopathy was in 2017.

- 95% of those polled either agreed or strongly agree that the term psychopath has a negative connotation to it.

- 15% of high school seniors strongly disagree with the statement that psychopathy is an inherited disorder and encoded in our genetics.

- 30% of students strongly agree with the statement that psychopathy is developed through our environment.

2

FIGURE 6–3 Thanks to the use of templates and examples I provided, Annabelle could focus on creating a professional-looking executive summary of her research findings about psychopathy.

KEY FINDING 2

95% of those polled either agreed or strongly agree that the term psychopath has a negative connotation to it.

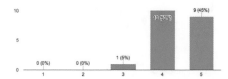

Building on the stigma that the word psychopath has an extremely negative connotation to it, it is also seen in the high school senior class. From movies, television series, and social media, these students have received this negative significance of the word. The percentage of students who strongly agree that "the term psychopath has a negative connotation to it" is just what I had expected to see from this survey, due to the stigma that we see all over the media in our world. This means that these students have seen something about psychopathy in their lives and it has left a lasting negative connotation in their lives.

FIGURE 6-3 Continued

KEY FINDING 1

Only 75% of high school seniors knew what the definition of psychopathy was in 2017.

- Personality disorder characterized by antisocial behavior, impaired empathy and remorse, egotistical traits.
- Personality disorder marked by alternating periods of elation and depression
- Crazy serial killers
- Other

High school seniors at Burlingame High School have become less aware of this disorder, which could result in many people being unaware of some dangers. Being that 15% are uninformed, the number is only bound to increase as time goes on and the disorder remains untalked about in our society.

Unlike the 75% who could identify the definition, there was a good 10% who confused bipolar disorder and psychopathy. I had intentionally done that in my survey to also see if students were informed on other disorders, and unfortunately that is the case here. Students are unable to distinguish separate disorders, and these disorders are in our community and school. This unawareness could potentially have a negative effect on many students and people all over.

3

KEY FINDING 3

15% of high school seniors strongly disagree with the statement that
psychopathy is an inherited disorder and encoded in our genetics.

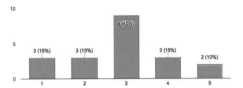

Students show slightly more diverse answers in this survey question. Some
strongly agree and some strongly disagree, but then there are some in the
middle. Majority of the students were in the middle and maybe unsure what
they believed. Maybe it was because they are uninformed on the topic so
they figured pick the middle would be the safest bet for them. The 15% that
disagreed with that statement must agree that environment shapes
psychopaths or some other claim that they have.

5

KEY FINDING 4

30% of students strongly agree with the statement that psychopathy is
developed through our environment.

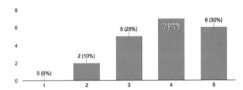

Although the last question had more diverse answers, this question leaned more towards
the agree or strongly agree side. In the middle there remains a good amount of
undecided maybe even uninformed people. No one had seemed to strongly disagree
with this statement. In the common "Nature v Nurture" debate, they would fall under the
nurture part because they believe environment can shape your personality. Many
students had agreed or strongly agreed, which, to say the least, surprised me. I thought
students would focus on the brain chemistry aspect of the disorder psychopathy.
Although turns out that there is much more diversity in the beliefs than I had expected.

6

FIGURE 6–3 Continued

Expert Project: Project Proposal
Mr. Burke/English IV 2016–17

Overview Please follow the guidelines, as they are meant to ensure your success on this assignment and teach you how to write a proposal, something many of you will have to do in one context or another. The directions and elements appear in the left column; the actual proposal should look *exactly like* the sample provided to the right. A clean (unannotated) version appears on the back.

ELEMENTS	EXAMPLE
Name Class Date	Katie Senior English IV September 16, 2015
Proposed subject you will study	**Subject:** Medical Evolution: Hearts: Trace hearts all the way back to Ancient Egypt and see what their function was thought to do. Then, trace hearts throughout the centuries and see how people's knowledge about them has changed. Find when the heart symbol came around and how its creation has changed the way people perceive hearts. Lastly, I want to take a medical approach to this topic and look at how heart surgery and medical research (blood pressure, diet, etc.) has evolved throughout the ages.
Questions to help you think about and explore this topic	**Questions:** What society was the first to acknowledge that hearts existed? What did people think their original function was? Where did the name heart come from (what is its origin)? When was the cardiovascular system discovered? Who created the heart symbol? What is it supposed to represent? What does it mean in today's society? How does it shape people's thoughts about hearts? Why do people associate the heart with feelings, when all it does is pump blood? Who first thought of operating on a heart? Who created the first technique? Who was the first surgeon to attempt an open heart surgery? Which surgeon was the first to successfully complete an open heart surgery? What was the first pacemaker made up of and what restrictions did they put on recipients' lives? How has the pacemaker's design and function changed as doctors have become more educated on the heart's function? How does age correlate to the success of heart surgery? How does diet correlate to heart disease and problems?
Rationale: Why do you want to study this topic? What is your rationale for investigating it?	**Rationale:** I have decided to research about hearts because they have always interested me since I was little. My little cousin was born with two holes in her heart and since then has had two open heart operations. This definitely was what piqued my interest in the study of hearts. One day I want to be a cardiothoracic surgeon so I think this topic is well suited for me. I find it interesting and it's broad enough of a topic to research for a year-long paper.
Summary: What are you investigating, how, and why?	**Summary:** I am investigating the heart muscle for this paper from its origins to the present. I will be tracing the heart muscle all the way back to times when it was thought of as the brain of a person. It will give me insight on how much people have learned about it and how this conclusion still affects the way people think about hearts today. Then, I want to research when the heart enigma came about and how people associate hearts with emotions. Then, I hope to go into explaining about how the cardiovascular system was discovered. I will go into detail about the first heart surgery and then go more into depth about the evolution of techniques. Finally, I will go into depth about heart health and diet. I will discuss different statistics about how America's heart facts compare to other countries. In the end I hope to write a good paper about both the evolution of the idea of hearts and the evolution of hearts in medicine.
Prediction of what you will learn from this investigation	**Prediction:** I predict that I will gain a lot of knowledge from the books I decided to read and the articles that I'll find. I will probably learn a lot of facts and will have to differentiate between what information is useful and what isn't. I predict that this is going to be fun to research, but also take a lot of dedication and hard work.
List of books you will read about this topic	**Reading and Resources** 1. *King of Hearts: The True Story of the Maverick Who Pioneered Open Heart Surgery*, G. Wayne Miller 2. *Black Man in a White Coat: A Doctor's Reflections on Race and Medicine*, Damon Tweedy 3. *Surgeon*, Atul Gawande 4. *The Man Who Touched His Own Heart: True Tales of Science, Surgery, and Mystery*, Rob Dunn
Explanation of the importance of this topic: So what? Who should care?	**Importance:** This topic is very important to me for personal reasons. But, also, because it is important to learn about heart health, especially since there are at least 1.5 million heart attacks in the US each year. Since this number will only keep growing, I think it is important to research the origins of the heart and all the findings after to try and educate myself and anyone who reads this paper about how to live a safe and healthy life.

FIGURE 6–4 The key elements of the design of this assignment are the annotations in the left margin explaining what students should do and the sample itself to show them how it should be formatted and written. *(continues)*

Example (Without Annotations)

Katie
Senior English IV
September 16, 2015

Subject: Medical Evolution: Hearts: Trace hearts all the way back to Ancient Egypt and see what their function was thought to do. Then, trace hearts throughout the centuries and see how people's knowledge about them has changed. Find when the heart symbol came around and how its creation has changed the way people perceive hearts. Lastly, I want to take a medical approach to this topic and look at how heart surgery and medical research (blood pressure, diet, etc.) has evolved throughout the ages.

Questions: What society was the first to acknowledge that hearts existed? What did people think their original function was? Where did the name heart come from (what is its origin)? When was the cardiovascular system discovered? Who created the heart symbol? What is it supposed to represent? What does it mean in today's society? How does it shape people's thoughts about hearts? Why do people associate the heart with feelings, when all it does is pump blood? Who first thought of operating on a heart? Who created the first technique? Who was the first surgeon to attempt an open heart surgery? Which surgeon was the first to successfully complete an open heart surgery? What was the first pacemaker made up of and what restrictions did they put on recipients' lives? How has the pacemaker's design and function changed as doctors have become more educated on the heart's function? How does age correlate to the success of heart surgery? How does diet correlate to heart disease and problems?

Rationale: I have decided to research about hearts because they have always interested me since I was little. My little cousin was born with two holes in her heart and since then has had two open heart operations. This definitely was what piqued my interest in the study of hearts. One day I want to be a cardiothoracic surgeon so I think this topic is well suited for me. I find it interesting and it's broad enough of a topic to research for a year-long paper.

Summary: I am investigating the heart muscle for this paper from its origins to the present. I will be tracing the heart muscle all the way back to times when it was thought of as the brain of a person. It will give me insight on how much people have learned about it and how this conclusion still affects the way people think about hearts today. Then, I want to research when the heart enigma came about and how people associate hearts with emotions. Then, I hope to go into explaining about how the cardiovascular system was discovered. I will go into detail about the first heart surgery and then go more into depth about the evolution of techniques. Finally, I will go into depth about heart health and diet. I will discuss different statistics about how America's heart facts compare to other countries. In the end I hope to write a good paper about both the evolution of the idea of hearts and the evolution of hearts in medicine.

Prediction: I predict that I will gain a lot of knowledge from the books I decided to read and the articles that I'll find. I will probably learn a lot of facts and will have to differentiate between what information is useful and what isn't. I predict that this is going to be fun to research, but also take a lot of dedication and hard work.

Reading and Resources
1. *King of Hearts: The True Story of the Maverick Who Pioneered Open Heart Surgery*, G. Wayne Miller
2. *Black Man in a White Coat: A Doctor's Reflections on Race and Medicine*, Damon Tweedy
3. *Surgeon*, Atul Gawande
4. *The Man Who Touched His Own Heart: True Tales of Science, Surgery, and Mystery*, Rob Dunn

Importance: This topic is very important to me for personal reasons. But, also, because it is important to learn about heart health, especially since there are at least 1.5 million heart attacks in the US each year. Since this number will only keep growing, I think it is important to research the origins of the heart and all the findings after to try and educate myself and anyone who reads this paper about how to live a safe and healthy life.

FIGURE 6–4 *Continued*

© 2019 by Jim Burke from *The Six Academic Writing Assignments*. Portsmouth, NH: Heinemann.

As you can see from the handout, the final result is not a long document; it is, however, a document in which every word and feature matters. I emphasize throughout the composition process of these proposals, which go through several rounds of revision, that when someone writes a proposal in the real world, those who read it will be looking for any reason to reject it. These proposals, and the survey and executive summary assignments, contribute to and thus are an essential part of the larger assignment of the Expert Project. As these alternative assignments remind us, we can improve the cohesion of our curriculum by looking for ways to link our different writing assignments so they can complement each other as these examples do.

Obstacles and Opportunities

One of the obstacles we most frequently encounter is the skeptical, sometimes resentful look in students' eyes about the value of what we want them to do, all of which is captured in that eternal challenge: "When will we ever use this?" It is this attitude that creates the opportunity for such assignments as I have discussed in this chapter. Central to the premise, of course, is that these assignments share a great deal of common ground with more traditional academic writing assignments in terms of the moves students must make as writers and thinkers.

As I said earlier in this chapter, many of the ideas for these assignments derive from the real world. The recurring emphasis on writing letters in my class, to different people for different reasons, stems from the realization of how many times I need to do this in my own life as an employee, customer, and citizen, examples of which I bring into class to show what such letters accomplished. And proposals? I realize now just how often we write them, though sometimes they appear as letters or must conform to some template provided by the agency in charge.

One obstacle we need to account for when designing alternative writing assignments is a lack of familiarity some may have with these forms, especially if they come from families or backgrounds that have had little experience with such writing. The students growing up in homes with parents who are in various professions will likely have some sense of these types of writing, especially those such as proposals and business letters; others, however, who are growing up in homes like the one I did, will have little cause to know about these forms or understand their importance. Thus we must keep explaining what students are doing, but also how to do it and why it matters—what advantages such knowledge and skills offer them.

More than anything, alternative writing assignments offer crucial solutions to the crisis of engagement we find ourselves facing so often. The first piece of writing I ever had published was a letter to the editor of the *Herald Tribune* protesting the bombing of Libya while I served in the Peace Corps in Tunisia. The first time I remember writing for a real purpose, with real passion, was not for my English class in high school, but, instead, to inform the student body that the administration had pulped an entire issue of the school newspaper (which I did not even write for!) over a story they wanted squelched. With a friend, I typed out our exposé as a call to action. Though I struggle to believe this myself, I, who was failing English (and a few other classes) at the time, casually strolled into the administrative office the next day, created a Ditto sheet, and ran off hundreds of copies as if I were merely a student aid. That night, while the administration enjoyed the evening and prepared for the next day, my friends and I distributed what we wrote around campus, taping all our remaining copies to the door of the administrative offices.

The young man (me) who was unwilling to do pretty much any of the assignments for pretty much any of my classes senior year was willing to write the exposé about the administration, detailed thank-you letters to guest speakers who had visited our English class, a business plan for the photography business I created senior year, and a résumé that initially ran to over ten pages, as it included every lawn I had ever mowed, every baby I had ever sat, every job I had ever had up to the age of seventeen. Though I laugh at the résumé experience, as did my mother and her friends when I showed it to them while they chatted in the kitchen one day, I also see in those ten pages the commitment to a task that was important because it was real. That spirit of engagement, the feeling that writing should be for real purposes to real people, that it can make a difference, can make things happen, is the reason that I design alternative writing assignments when I can and that I regularly bring into the class examples of writing from the real world that demonstrate and remind students of its importance. One example of such a piece of writing is the local real estate report published by Raziel Ungar, a former student of mine, who understands the importance of being able to communicate complex ideas using clear language, images, data, and stories. Raziel regularly publishes, in print and online, profiles of the community, new properties, and the people who live in the area. In these reports, he includes professional photographs of the people to complement the stories he tells about them and the community in which they bought a house. The stories include charts, tables, and other images that help him make his point, tell his story—and, of course, grow his business.

His real estate reports are a wonderful extension of the work Raziel did when, as a high school student seeking his Eagle Scout status, he decided to write an extended history of Burlingame, his hometown and the town where I have taught all these years, for his Eagle Project. His work, then as a student and now as a successful real estate agent, illustrates the importance and opportunities of the sort of assignments discussed in this chapter. If only we could find a way to create badges for writing, our students might work as hard for them as Boy Scouts do for their own merit badges.

Reflect on Your Own Practice

Consider the different types of alternative assignments I have discussed in this chapter and how they compare with your own classroom and curriculum. Specifically, I suggest that you do the following steps in your head, in writing, or as part of a discussion with members of your department or those instructional teams (sometimes called PLCs) to which you belong.

1. Generate a list of all the different alternative assignments you have students do in a semester or during a specific unit you just finished or are about to begin. You might take a minute to examine the assumptions behind these different assignments or the degree to which they complement other, larger assignments in your overall curriculum. Make notes as needed about ways you could improve your use or the design of alternative assignments based on your observations.

2. Examine the assignments on the list you created or a smaller subset of representative assignments in light of the AWA Framework checklist to assess the degree to which these writing assignments include or could be improved to better incorporate the features listed on the AWA Framework.

Conclusion

Teaching Writing Better by Design

> *Design thinking starts with divergence, the deliberate attempt*
> *to expand the range of options rather than narrow them.*
>
> —TIM BROWN, *Change by Design*

Design Teams: Creating a Culture of Collaboration

Alternative
View of
the Design
Thinking
Model

Throughout this book, we have examined the idea of the teacher as designer and students as users of the assignments we design, the lessons we teach, the classrooms and communities we create. Though some use different terms, the design thinking process I have featured here has the following elements: empathize, define, ideate, prototype, and test. The assignments and ideas I have shared with you throughout this book have all moved through these design stages many times on their way to becoming a working part of the curriculum in my senior English class. But they have not gone through this process in the dark recesses of my office where I worked into the late hours by myself.

Collaboration is fundamental to the design process at each stage. What you have seen throughout the book are assignments that grew out of conversations between the senior English teachers at my school, sometimes online, other times during our dedicated PLC meeting time on Wednesday mornings. What followed from those initial discussions was aligned with the design process as we proceeded, checking in with each other through meetings, text messages, or visits to each other's classes to discuss how some part of the writing assignment went that day. Then we continued on or refined as needed based on students' response to the assignment, moving through a long series of junctures, each one of which had three choices: proceed, revise, or stop. Our senior team, however, is long-established and comfortable with throwing out ideas or challenging those same ideas. We call each other with ideas; we call each other out if we have questions about anyone's ideas. When we arrive at a working draft of an assignment, the senior team usually asks me to "Burkify it!" by which they mean write it up and format it according to the guidelines of the framework spelled out in this book. Our senior team works. We listen. We lament. We learn. We laugh. But it took some years to get to this place.

But what about those design teams that have yet to become a team, where people nod and nod and then retreat to their rooms, where they engage in their own private practices? What about the teachers, especially the new teachers, in the group who do not feel welcome or able to speak, to propose, to question? These hard but essential conversations are also a vital part of the design process, the moments when teachers should feel free to advocate for ideas or voice their reservations about some aspect of the writing assignment but often do not. I have observed passionate, committed teachers lobby against legitimate writing assignments they thought were too difficult or simply too much work given the other demands of their lives at that moment. I have seen similar conversations dominated by equally committed teachers who argued for pushing students up to and beyond the "perspiration point," saying that such high expectations were the only way these students would accomplish all that the teachers knew they could, if they were only given the right conditions and the right assignment.

These are the sort of challenging parts of the design process that can, if guided by an effective team or department leader, bring about a deeper change in the structure and culture of the department as a whole. These are the sort of "hard conversations" Jen Abrams refers to when she writes, "A thousand things are unspoken in schools every day, and the lack of truth telling enforces an ineffective status quo. Change—personal and institutional—requires that we speak out loud about what we know and believe. We need to be liberated from those of our beliefs that limit us. We need to find our voice around what matters most" (2009, xii).

Jennifer Abrams' Website and Resources for "Hard Conversations"

Even this idea of "what matters most," which Abrams implies we should all know and accept, is part of the scrum of these sorts of conversations. I cannot remember a time in my career when we have felt compelled to consider so many different constraints and factors when designing writing assignments—gender, safe spaces, sociopolitical tensions, standards, socioeconomic status, state assessments, race, culture, English learners, special needs, emotional and mental health, generational dispositions, technology, attention, and so many more. Yet these are part of the hard conversation we are all learning to have with ourselves and the members of our design or department teams.

When we sit down to design these assignments, to chart these journeys for ourselves and our students, it is important that we do so in good faith, willing to have the conversations that each assignment demands of us. What's more, such occasions provide an invaluable apprenticeship for the newer teachers who need to learn how to participate in such conversations and to realize that they do, in fact, have valid contributions to make throughout the design process. These new teachers, whether new to the team or the department, are also *users* of these assignments; however, because they were not present at the conception of some unit, they often receive the assignments and all their handouts with little guidance and no real room to make these assignments their own in some meaningful way. Trying to teach a unit others developed is, for most teachers, similar to putting together furniture from IKEA; it's difficult to use others' materials and methods to teach writing. But it is problematic for another reason: It prevents the teachers from feeling any sense of ownership, undermines their investment in the unit or writing assignment, and effectively excludes them and their voice from the assignment.

To foster a conversation and culture of collaboration, it is vital that assignments, as with these assignments I have shared with you, not be treated as though they were written in stone. How could they be when the kids and conditions we work with change so much each year? When the constraints within which we work change every year in subtle but substantive ways that inevitably affect what we do and how we do it? When world events demand that we move that *1984* unit up to the fall during the election year? When we suddenly have a class set of Chromebooks to use every day and are challenged to use them in ways that will make a difference? When the unit that challenged all students so well last year challenges so few this year? And sometimes we get all these variations packed into one year, so it seems as if we are teaching, as I did one year, completely different classes. Yet we cannot create separate assignments for three different classes. We can, however, as you see in many of the assignments throughout the book, allow students meaningful choices so that they can challenge themselves at the level appropriate to their current performance and thereby increase their level of engagement.

Continuum of Engagement

Nor can—or should—we try to create new academic writing assignments each year in response to these constant changes. Yet some do, driven by their own need for novelty; however, novelty, it turns out, can sometimes be an unwelcome friction point for many. Same goes for that "incredible idea" for a new paper for the *Kite Runner* unit I had on the way to work at sixty-five mph while listening to my favorite podcast. While the design thinking process permits all such ideas to be thrown into the idea pile, it demands greater discipline from us, imposes on us a level of intentionality when it comes to designing and refining our writing assignments. A careful examination of the different writing assignments spelled out in the preceding chapters would reveal that nearly all these are in their fourth, sixth, or even tenth version.

As a result of this more dedicated prototyping and testing cycle, I spend less time each year creating new assignments and more time improving the ones we have created and used in the past. Through this recursive process of ongoing improvement, our senior design team can focus on teaching the skills needed for the assignment and providing better support to our students by revising the assignment handouts, gathering a range of student examples, and assembling additional resources they can use in class or online. In recent years, with class sets of Chromebooks in our classrooms, the senior team has devoted much of is energy to adapting more of the assignments and support resources for online use, a transition that comes with many new possibilities and problems that we will eventually resolve.

Friction Points: What They Are and Why They Matter

Reading through the preceding chapters, reflecting on the different types of writing assignments and how they play out in your own classroom, you have no doubt wondered about certain things that were not the primary focus of this book but for a working teacher would be important to know.

One of recurring ideas throughout the book is that of friction points and how we should think about them when designing assignments. When our aim is to facilitate and deepen learning, friction is something to embrace, to intentionally integrate into the lesson or, in this case, the writing assignment. By adding or increasing relevant friction, or what Dirksen, in *Design for How People Learn*, calls the "germane cognitive load," we make the learning more sticky and enhance comprehension (2016, 167). In short, this type of friction demands that the student make his or her own connections; the student has to handle the cognitive load of the tasks. So anything you ask students to do that forces them to digest or interact with the material they are trying to learn is the sort of productive friction we should be cultivating into our assignments, handouts, and class instruction.

If "good" friction helps people learn and retain the content, "bad" friction disrupts the user's experience, thereby preventing or at least diminishing learning and deeper connections. Victoria Young (n.d.) describes the effects of such bad friction in an article about the user's journey as it relates to interface in technology design:

> In user experience, friction is defined as interactions that inhibit people from intuitively and painlessly achieving their goals within a digital interface. Friction is a major problem because it leads to bouncing, reduces conversions, and frustrates would-be customers to the point of abandoning their tasks. Today, the most successful digital experiences have emerged out of focusing on reducing friction in the user journey. The strategic design decisions these companies have made have exponentially accelerated user adoption and engagement.

In case I have not made it clear, I am suggesting that we recognize and treat our handouts, materials, and any other means of instructing our students as interfaces in the same way apps, websites, and devices are. In other words, each of these things has a use—serves a purpose—which its design either facilitates or undermines. When we choose a means, a method, or a medium, we are creating an interface that is part of the user's journey. We must now consider this interface an integral part of students' experience of our class and curriculum, both of which they *use* as students in the same way we use a business and its services or a website and its content.

When it comes to designing writing assignments, the bad friction points come in several different forms, some more conspicuous than others. First, we can all do our part, at both the individual and the departmental or institutional level, to realize the dream of a common language among teachers, one that is clear and consistent in its usage and meaning, when writing assignments or teaching reading and writing. Language that is unclear or otherwise confusing to students slows them down and undermines their performance, leaving students to wonder why we can't all get together as teachers and agree to certain terms and truths. So, too, do all the competing versions of MLA guides and rubrics floating around the average department. To this end, we have worked to establish a common MLA department style guide and rubric for argument papers. Additional negative friction points amount to anything that impedes readability and usability of the handouts or the assignment as a whole. This might include formatting or features but could also have to do with the diction or the means by which the assignment or related support documents are displayed, accessed, or used.

Returning for a moment to that day in the copy room where this whole inquiry began, I found document design a constant source of friction for many students once I began analyzing handouts for writing assignments across disciplines. Though the language of the documents, as mentioned earlier, was an issue in many instances, I am speaking here about such features as the layout, the fonts, and the formatting. When we violate the rules of effective writing that we are trying to teach—with random or excessive use of fun fonts, exclamation points, bold, italics, all caps, and color, to name a few—we increase the number of friction points that can make it difficult to understand or complete the assignment. When our documents are unreadable because so much information has been crowded onto a page, with no clear way to navigate it, we are the source of much of the trouble. When we distribute our documents digitally, but by means or in formats that are neither intuitive nor clear to our student users, we must accept some responsibility for any subsequent complications or confusion from students. By thinking like designers when creating not only the assignments but the means by which we convey and support those assignments, we are likely to achieve, as Young says in her remarks about friction, "exponentially accelerated user adoption and engagement" from our students, to borrow the language of interface design for a moment.

Document Design Checklist

The Paper Load: Collecting, Responding to, and Grading the Writing Assignments

The selection of means and media, when it comes to creating, collecting, and responding to writing assignments, grows more crucial for us all as we navigate the growing number of digital options. Do I create and distribute the document in Google Docs or as a pdf? Do I distribute and display it on paper or a screen—or both? What functionality does going digital allow? Or would that just add another set of potentially problematic friction points? And when I distribute the actual writing assignment document digitally, do I use Google Classroom, a Google Doc shared link, Blackboard Learn, Canvas, or something more specific to my class, such as the Daily Record? Then when it comes time to collect the writing assignment, do I go with paper or only digital? If only digital, do I, again, decide to choose Google Classroom, Google Drive, Canvas, or something like Turnitin? These are not simple questions, for according to a 2015 report from Common Sense Media, the average teenager spends nine hours a day looking at screens of one sort or another; our decision to add to that time has real implications for both our students and ourselves.

Daily Record

The point here is to remember that what we choose—paper or digital—determines how we will work with and be able to respond to students and their writing. If I require students to submit their finished papers to Turnitin, I am locking myself into many more hours a day looking at screens. I am also deciding how I will read and respond to students' papers, given that Turnitin, for example, offers a specific set of tools I can use. As we move toward artificial intelligence through such AI instruments as Turnitin's Revision Assistant, we will increasingly face the decision as to whether to design the writing assignment to be read and responded to by the teacher or by the algorithms embedded in Revision Assistant or other such services that are no doubt part of our future.

How I respond to the assignments obviously depends on which of the six different types a given assignment is. As I discussed in the chapters on writing to learn and short answers, these are not assignments that students are revising, as one would a process paper, for example, so the response is typically quick, with suggestions about how to improve on such work in the future. When possible and appropriate, however, I try to include opportunities to improve on such WTL assignments as the daybook; to that end, as I mentioned in the WTL chapter, the daybook grade for the second grading period *replaces* the grade they had for the first grading period, and so it goes with the third and final grading period. Instead of them having three major grades for the daybook, I want them to feel they can work to improve their ability to use writing to learn. Of course if some student tries to cheat the system and gets Fs on the first two grading periods for his daybook but does a great job for the last six weeks, we will have a conversation about why a C would be the highest possible grade that daybook could receive.

Aside from my efforts to incorporate feedback into the papers through peer response and conferences with me in class, I respond in two different modes: explaining why they got the grade they did and detailing what they can do to improve their paper when they revise. The first type of response, explaining the grade, is primarily accomplished through checklists or scoring guides. I will often identify common patterns of error or trouble across all papers and then discuss those patterns as a class, showing students examples to illustrate. My main method of feedback for some years now has been to use the Voice Memo app on my iPhone or the audio recording feature in Turnitin's Feedback Assistant. Which one I use to provide feedback on a student's paper depends on the importance and size of the paper and whether the student will be able to revise. Turnitin allows only three minutes of audio feedback; my Voice Memo app gives me as long as I want, though I have found that I can send the audio file as an attachment to a student's email only if it is under eight minutes. This ability to respond to students' writing has been transformative, allowing me to effectively hold a one-sided personal conference with each student. I find it far less stressful and more satisfying than writing on students' papers.

Writing brings us into contact with our students in ways few other subjects do. Most students feel very vulnerable and anxious about their writing, even writing that is not personal. Throughout the book, I have emphasized the need for meaningful writing assignments, for assignments that form a cohesive and logical progression over the course of the year. For what we are really doing when we create a year's worth of writing assignments, of *experiences*, is designing a story. Each day's class is a sentence, each week a paragraph, each unit a chapter in the story of the year students spend in our classes. And as with any good story, there needs to be tension and transformation by the time one arrives at the end, or what I have called the "user's journey" throughout this book. Though an overly familiar phrase, we are nonetheless teaching students how to "enter the conversation" of our discipline, especially as writers, who are engaged in the hard work of learning not only to compose their papers but themselves, each assignment doing its part to help them craft the next draft of themselves.

References

Abrams, Jennifer. 2009. *Having Hard Conversations.* Thousand Oaks, CA: Sage.

Adhikary, Amrita. 2009. "Mapping a Designer: Henry Dreyfuss." *Design History Mashup* (blog). September 10. http://designhistorymashup.blogspot.com/2009/09/mapping -designer-henry-dreyfuss.html. Accessed August 24, 2017.

Applebee, Arthur N., Anne Auten, and Fran Lehr. 1981. *Writing in the Secondary School: English and the Content Areas.* National Council of Teaches of English.

Applebee, Arthur N., and Judith Langer. 2013. *Writing Instruction That Works: Proven Methods for Middle and High School Classrooms.* New York: Teachers College Press/ National Writing Project.

Atwell, Nancie. 2003. "Hard Trying and These Recipes." *Voices from the Middle* 11 (2): 16–19.

Bautista, Mark, Melanie Bertrand, Ernest Morrell, D'Artagnan Scorza, and Corey Matthews. 2013. "Participatory Action Research and City Youth: Methodological Insights from the Council of Youth Research." *Teachers College Record* 115 (10): 1–23.

Beck, Isabel L., and Margaret G. McKeown. 2006. *Improving Comprehension with Question the Author: A Fresh and Expanded View of a Powerful Approach.* New York: Scholastic.

Booth, Wayne, Gregory Colomb, Joseph M. Williams, Joseph Bizup, and William T. Fitzgerald. 2016. *The Craft of Research.* 4th edition. Chicago Guides to Writing, Editing, and Publishing. Chicago: University of Chicago.

Brown, Tim. 2009. *Change by Design: How Design Thinking Transforms Organizations and Inspires Innovation.* New York: Harper Business.

Burke, Jim. 2013. *The Common Core Companion: The Standards Decoded, Grades 9–12: What They Say, What They Mean, How to Teach Them.* Thousand Oaks, CA: Corwin Literacy.

———. 2017a. *Uncharted Territory: A High School Reader.* New York: W. W. Norton.

———. 2017b. *Your Literacy Standards Companion: What They Mean and How to Teach Them.* Thousand Oaks, CA: Corwin Literacy.

College Board. 2014. *Test Specifications for the Redesigned SAT*. New York: College Board.

———. 2016. *AP Seminar: Course and Exam Description (Part of the AP Capstone Program)*. Rev. edition. New York: College Board.

Common Sense Media. 2015. "Landmark Report: U.S. Teens Use an Average of Nine Hours of Media per Day, Tweens Use Six Hours." November 3. www.common sensemedia.org. Accessed January 4, 2018.

Council of Writing Program Administrators, National Council of Teachers of English, and the National Writing Project. 2011. *Framework for Success in Postsecondary Writing*. Rochester, MI, Urbana, IL, and Berkeley, CA: Council of Writing Program Administrators, National Council of Teachers of English, and the National Writing Project. www.ncte.org/positions/statements/collwritingframework/.

Cox, Rebecca D. 2009. *The College Fear Factor: How Students and Professors Misunderstand One Another*. Cambridge, MA: Harvard University Press.

Creger, John. 2014–15. "The Personal Creed Project: Portal to Deepened Learning." *Journal for Expanded Perspectives on Learning* 20 (winter): 60–73.

Dirksen, Julie. 2016. *Design for How People Learn*. 2nd edition. San Francisco: New Riders.

Dweck, Carol S. 2006. *Mindset: The New Psychology of Success*. Ballantine Books: New York.

Duncan-Andrade, Jeffrey M., and Ernest Morrell. 2008. *The Art of Critical Pedagogy: Possibilities for Moving from Theory to Practice in Urban Schools*. New York: Peter Lang.

Egan, Kieran. 2010. *Learning in Depth: A Simple Innovation That Can Transform Schooling*. Chicago: University of Chicago.

Fisher, Douglas, and Nancy Frey. 2014. *Text-Dependent Questions, Grades 6–12: Pathways to Close and Critical Reading*. Thousand Oaks, CA: Corwin.

Fister, Barbara. 2011. "Burke's Parlor Tricks: Introducing Research as Conversation." *Library Babel Fish* (blog). November 11. www.insidehighered.com/blogs/library-babel -fish/burkes-parlor-tricks-introducing-research-conversation.

Fitzhugh, Will. 2017. "Writing Is in a 'Skills' Rut." *The Concord Review*. June 19. http://theconcordreview.blogspot.com/2017/06/writing-is-in-skills-rut.html. Accessed June 19, 2017.

Flanagan, Linda. 2017. "How Schools Can Help Students Develop a Greater Sense of Purpose." *Mind/Shift* (blog). May 2. https://ww2.kqed.org/mindshift/2017/05/02/how-schools-can-help-students-develop-a-greater-sense-of-purpose. Accessed July 28, 2017.

Forsman, Syrene. 1985. "Writing to Learn Means Learning to Think." In *Roots in the Sawdust: Writing to Learn Across the Disciplines,* ed. A. R. Gere, 162–74. Urbana, IL: National Council of Teachers of English.

French, John R. P. Jr., and Bertram H. Raven. 1959. "The Bases of Social Power." In *Studies in Social Power*, ed. D. Cartwright, 150–67. Ann Arbor, MI: Institute for Social Research.

Fulwiler, Toby, and Art Young. 1982. Introduction. In *Language Connections: Writing and Reading Across the Curriculum, ed.* Toby Fulwiler and Art Young, ix–xiii. Urbana, IL: National Council of Teachers of English.

Gallagher, Kelly. 2010. "Reversing Readicide." *Educational Leadership* 67 (6): 36–41.

Golding, William. 1954. *Lord of the Flies*. Faber and Faber: London.

Graff, Gerald, and Cathy Birkenstein. 2014. *They Say/I Say: The Moves That Matter in Academic Writing*. High school edition. New York: W. W. Norton.

Harvey, Gordon. 2009. "A Brief Guide to the Elements of the Academic Essay." Harvard College Writing Program. https://writingproject.fas.harvard.edu/files/hwp/files/hwp_brief_guides_elements.pdf.

Hasso Plattner Institute of Design at Stanford University. n.d. "The Design Thinking Process." Redesigning Theater. http://web.stanford.edu/group/cilab/cgi-bin/redesigningtheater/the-design-thinking-process/. Accessed May 23, 2016.

Hattie, John. 2009. *Visible Learning: A Synthesis of Over 800 Meta-Analyses Relating to Achievement*. New York: Routledge.

Johnson, Christopher. 2011. *Microstyle: The Art of Writing Little*. New York: W. W. Norton.

Kittle, Penny. 2018. Home page. Penny Kittle: Teacher–Author–Advocate. http://pennykittle.net. Accessed August 12, 2017.

Krakauer, Jon. 1996. *Into the Wild*. New York: Villard.

Langer, Ellen. 2014. *Mindfulness*. 25th ann. edition. Boston: Da Capo.

Langer, Judith. 2000. *Beating the Odds: Teaching Middle and High School Students to Read and Write Well*. CELA Research Report Number 12014. Rev. edition. Albany, NY: National Research Center on English Learning and Achievement.

Levine, Mel. 2004. *The Myth of Laziness*. New York: Simon and Schuster.

Melzer, Dan. 2014. *Assignments from Across the Curriculum: A National Study of College Writing*. Logan: Utah State University Press.

Murray, Donald M. 2005. *Write to Learn*. 8th edition. Boston: Thomson/Wadsworth.

Newkirk, Thomas. 2016. "Seeing Anew: An Invitation to Teacher Research." In *Heinemann 2016–2017 Professional Development Catalog-Journal*, 6–9. Portsmouth, NH: Heinemann.

Olson, Carol Booth, Robin C. Scarcella, and Tina Matuchniak. 2015. *Helping English Learners to Write: Meeting Common Core Standards, Grades 6–12*. New York: Teachers College Press.

Oppong, Thomas. 2017. "The Life-Changing Habit of Journaling (Why Einstein, Leonardo da Vinci, and Many More Great Minds Recommend It)." *Thrive Global* (blog). https://medium.com/thrive-global/start-journaling-54ea2edb104. Accessed June 22, 2017.

Orwell, George. 1949. *1984*. Secker & Warburg: London.

Page, Lily. 2017. "After a Year of Research, Senior Expert Projects Come to a Close." *Burlingame B*. April 21, 3.

Pépin, Jacques. 2016. "Newshour Essay: Jacques Pépin Says Following a Recipe Can Lead to Disaster." *PBS Newshour*. April 13.

Prose, Francine. 2006. *Reading Like a Writer: A Guide for People Who Love Books and for Those Who Want to Write Them*. New York: Harper Collins.

Rafael, Taffy E., Kathy Highfield, and Kathryn H. Au. 2006. *QAR Now: Question-Answer Relationships: A Powerful and Practical Framework That Develops Comprehension and Higher-Level Thinking in All Students*. New York: Scholastic.

Robinson, Bill. n.d. "Reading and Writing." http://jonsenglishsite.info/Pedagogy%20articles/Download%20PDF%20and%20Word/Read_&_Write_Robinson.pdf. Accessed May 15, 2016.

Romano, Tom. 2013. *Fearless Writing: Multigenre to Motivate and Inspire*. Portsmouth, NH: Heinemann.

Rose, Mike, and Malcolm Kiniry. 1997. *Critical Strategies for Academic Thinking and Writing*. 3d edition. Boston: Bedford.

Rothstein, Dan, and Luz Santana. 2011. *Make Just One Change: Teach Students to Ask Their Own Questions*. Cambridge, MA: Harvard Education Press.

Russell, David. 1991. *Writing in the Academic Disciplines, 1870–1990: A Curricular History*. Carbondale, IL: Southern Illinois University Press.

Santelises, Sonja Brookins, and Joan Dabrowski. 2015. *Checking In: Do Classroom Assignments Reflect Today's Higher Standards?* Washington, DC: Education Trust.

Shanahan, Tim. 2017. "How Do You Make a Good Reader? Just the Basics." *Shanahan on Literacy* (blog). http://shanahanonliteracy.com/blog/how-do-you-make-a-good -reader-just-the-basics#sthash.zNCXf1rz.dpbs. Accessed May 21, 2017.

Singer, Natasha. 2017. "Silicon Valley Courts Brand-Name Teachers, Raising Ethics Issues." *New York Times*. September 2.

Skloot, Rebecca. 2011. *The Immortal Life of Henrietta Lacks.* New York: Broadway Books.

Sommers, Nancy. 2012. "Becoming a College Writer: Learning to Revise." *Between the Drafts: Nancy Sommers's Teaching Journal* (blog). January 30. https://bedfordbits .colostate.edu/index.php/2012/01/30/becoming-a-college-writer-learning-to-revise/. Accessed June 25, 2016.

Tatum, Alfred. 2005. *Teaching Reading to Black Adolescent Males: Closing the Achievement Gap*. Portland, ME: Stenhouse.

Ulin, David L. 2010. *The Lost Art of Reading: Why Books Matter in a Distracted Time*. Seattle: Sasquatch Books.

Wilhelm, Jeffrey D., Michael W. Smith, and James E. Fredericksen. 2012. *Get It Done! Writing and Analyzing Informational Texts to Make Things Happen (Exceeding the Common Core)*. Portsmouth, NH: Heinemann.

Wilhoit, Stephen. 2002. *The Allyn and Bacon Teaching Assistant's Handbook*. New York: Longman.

Yang, K. Wayne, and Jeff Duncan-Andrade. 2006. "Doc Ur Block." Education for Liberation Network. Burke_6_WHOLE_BK_EDITED.docxwww.edliberation.org /resources/lab/records/doc-ur-block. Accessed July 22, 2017.

Young, Victoria. n.d. "Strategic UX: The Art of Reducing Friction." *Telepathy* (blog). www.dtelepathy.com/blog/business/strategic-ux-the-art-of-reducing-friction.

Index

language. *See also* writing process
  common, developing with teaching
    teams, 160
  concise and readable in assignments, 8,
    44, 79
  confusing, as source of friction, 160
laptops. *See* computers, laptops
letters, as form of alternative writing, 140
Lexi (student), independent reading work,
    124
Listener's Notes tool, 27, 58
literature, extended papers on, 88, 113, 118
Lord of the Flies (Golding), short-answer
    assignments for, 49–50
Lucas (student), reflections on the Expert
    Project, 132–33
Lunsford, Andrea and Karen, 112

major papers. *See* academic writing; Expert
    Project; extended papers
Mandell, Lindsey (student), self-assessment
    of process paper, 94
McAlindon, Annabelle (student), Primary
    Research Summary: Report and Inter-
    pretations of Findings, 148–50
Melzer, Dan
  on extended writing experience, 112
  research on writing assignments, 5
  on short-answer exams and writing as-
    signments, 16, 48–49
metacognition, 117
Michael (student)
  "Death of Freedom" essay, 107–8
  on revising process papers, 104–5
micromessages, 146
Microsoft Word, comments feature, 40
Microstyle: The Art of Writing Little (John-
    son), 144–47
Mikka (student), audio essay, 142–43

minilessons
  on aspects of writing process, 91–92
  as opportunity for feedback, 106
  on writing critically about unusual text
    forms, 122–24
MLA department style guide, 160
Montaigne, Michel de, 24
multimedia presentations
  as alternative writing form, 4, 137, 140
  as part of the Expert Project, 130–31
Murray, Donald, 33

National Council of Teachers of English
    (NCTE), Framework for Success in
    Postsecondary Writing, Framework for
    Success in Postsecondary Writing, 117
Newkirk, Tom, 2
Nick (student)
  draft of process paper, 107
  reflection on the Field assignment, 16
1984 (Orwell)
  approaching using the Digital Daybook, 33–34
  example short-answer questions for, 62–63
  WTL assignments related to, 34–37
nonfiction texts. *See also* Expert Project; *Into
    the Wild* (Krakauer); research paper as-
    signment; *The Immortal Life of Henrietta
    Lacks* (Skloot)
  close reading, 69, 128
  for independent reading, 73–74
  for simulated research assignment, 74
note-taking
  hand written notes, 37–38, 78
  tools and techniques for, 25–27
  in WTL assignments, student views on, 17

Objectives section (process paper assign-
    ments), 96–98
openness to new ideas, 117